Kingdom Publishers

Voice in the Wilderness

Copyright © Linda Plant

All rights reserved. No part of this book may be reproduced in any form by photocopying or any electronic or mechanical means, including information storage or retrieval systems, without permission in writing from both the copyright owner and the publisher of the book. The right of Linda Plant to be identified as the author of this work has been asserted by her in accordance with the Copyright, Designs and Patents Act 1988 and any subsequent amendments thereto. A catalogue record for this book is available from the British Library.

All Scripture Quotations have been taken from the New International Version and the King James Version of the Bible.

ISBN: 978-1-913247-87-4

1st Edition by Kingdom Publishers
Kingdom Publishers
London, UK.

You can purchase copies of this book from any leading bookstore or email
contact@kingdompublishers.co.uk

"A voice cries in the wilderness, prepare the way of the Lord;
make straight in the desert a highway for our God.
⁴Every valley shall be lifted up,
and every mountain and hill be made low;
the uneven ground shall become level,
and the rough places a plain.
⁵And the glory of the Lord shall be revealed,
and all flesh shall see it together,
for the mouth of the Lord has spoken."

Isaiah 40 v3 -5 (ESV)

AUTHOR PREVIEW ~ THE TREASURES OF DARKNESS

My previous published book, Grace to my Soul, was written mainly in the late 1970's while I was following a pathway of faith discovery. As such when completed, the book was for one reason or another relegated to a cupboard. In truth I had no idea what to do with it, or who would possibly be interested in my writing?

Never-the-less through the following years I did not actually ever stop writing. Always the moving of the Holy Spirit came to speak and illuminate the word of God and from that I would write down my inner thoughts. Mostly these were kept in journals and notebooks, where I would quite simply imprint my conversations with our Lord.

Moving forward, if you are now to look into the pages of my next book, A Voice in the Wilderness; much time has elapsed. Alongside the passing of that time, huge it seems to us as we measure these things! In God and the eternal workings of grace it is but a flicker, a moment like the blink of an eye.

This journey has been set in eternal time and all that will unfold along the way requires our full and complete co-operation. 'A Voice in the Wilderness' covers a period of time that was, a most wonderful overflowing blessing and also the deepest most devastating time my husband and I have ever been required to face.

As with the dreams of Pharaoh, to which Joseph was gifted with the interpretation; the good years gave way to terrible darkness beyond our ability to cope. It is so important to state that all the writing that you will find in this book and those following onwards, was as a direct result of the hand of God which never fails nor leaves His own abandoned by the roadside.

It is also of vital importance to make the statement that we were, I was, unable to stand in the vicious storm that blew upon our lives. The writing therefore from this period is retrospective as I was only able to see clearly to form anything of sense or expression in a further period. It is so often the case that while we battle with the wind and the waves, struggling to keep our little boat afloat; our visibility is restricted and we are almost entirely preoccupied with surviving the storm! So it was as I began to emerge from the worst of the tempest which had overtaken our lives, gradually I began to see and understand the essence of what God had accomplished. How it is when we are in the middle of a terrible storm, that which we see and even know is shrouded by mist and bitter winds.

Today so much is spoken about being strong for God, standing in the storms that come, lifting our hands in praise when everything around us lies in shreds! Well great if you can, but here is I consider a better way, allow the arms of Jesus to be your strength, your bold stay.

Thus says the LORD to his anointed, to Cyrus,
whose right hand I have grasped,
to subdue nations before him
and to lose the belts of kings,
to open doors before him
that gates may not be closed:

[2]**"I will go before you**
and level the exalted places,
I will break in pieces the doors of bronze
and cut through the bars of iron,

> **[3]I will give you the treasures of darkness
> and the hoards in secret places,
> that you may know that it is I, the LORD,
> the God of Israel, who call you by your name**
>
> **Isaiah 45 v 1-3 (ESV)**

So it is that the writing of this book did not happen as we struggled with terrible distress in bold and certain faith, rather it was like a man hanging by finger tips over a cliff. It is so important to be real and also to allow the workings of time to have their imprint upon our emotional trauma. Rather as the years progressed there was a realisation that a way had been travelled and it was Jesus who had thus carried us beyond where we knew!

Gradually I saw that the situation did not change, the difficulties were not miraculously solved, rather I was different and He had worked that. The treasures of darkness has always resonated with me and now I see how it is that He takes our deepest darkest times, weaving them with heavenly cords of love and we discover a treasure beyond our expectation. So it is that the writing to be found in this book follows a way of stumbling through very dark times, until we realise that He never ever left us and kept us throughout it all. The overriding requirement for this to happen is not great bounding faith, though something of that is always helpful! Rather it is to be submitted to Him and Him alone, being prepared to give up and yield and yield, and still yield further and further.

Doubt and despair will be familiar travelling companions to lure away a broken heart, how sensible would it be to allow bitterness to continue on unabated? We cannot and sometimes it takes a real effort to refuse to allow, the awful negative distress to have the last word! In the wilderness place, where every other normal contact of faith and church was removed a 'special something' was birthed. That 'something' brought forth a voice to speak from a barren and empty place, it is **'a voice in the wilderness!'**

DEDICATION

To those who serve, giving of their lives and their substance for the joy of Him, who is their Lord Jesus Christ. Also for those, who for one reason or another find themselves to be abandoned and alone, with the anticipation that in these pages hope will be reborn.

ACKNOWLEDGEMENTS

In thankfulness for those brave souls, who continued to love, care and give support, when the boat of our lives became cast upon the rocks of adversity. Sadly it is, that so many whose lives, a beacon were to us, of the life of faith, evaporated into the grey mist, when the storm winds gathered.

In the fullness of Jesus Christ, as His church, there are those who have persevered with love to lift the falling soul and maintain those who found themselves alone and abandoned in rolling seas.

PREMISE

We take the road of faith as we journey onwards through life. Having found our Lord and Saviour, Jesus Christ the pathway opens up ahead of us as the light of heaven streams across our way. Wonderful it is and glorious as the eager steps of first faith bring confidence and assurance.

However life is never going to only bring sunny days, all the seasons of nature provide for us a pattern and a sequence to which our very existence revolves around. Winter brings forth the new growth of springtime, this is the rhythm of life.

For the Christian there is no promise that the sun will always shine and that winter winds will be kept from our experience. We set out upon a great adventure of faith, it is a journey of life and perhaps the turning of the road will be much different that we could have ever expected!

For us, this was a journey set in God's calling and answered faithfully. The outworking of that journey, would we have still made, had we known the terrible cost it would inflict upon our lives? Oh, yes we would still make the same choice, even now! The call, is all that counts. We respond to His will and His purposes. It is a privilege to walk upon the beautiful pathway, which is a service to our Lord Jesus Christ, no matter what!

CONTENTS

1. Forward
2. Introduction
3. A New Well
4. The Place of Vision
5. The Waterfall of Grace
6. Heavenly Encounter
7. Write the Vision
8. The Dark Journey
9. Burnout!
10. The Oil and the Wine
11. Its all Right to be Cast Out
12. A Voice in the Wilderness
13. Addendum to the Dark Journey
14. Where is the Water Level?
15. No Compromise
16. Riding the Wave/ Eddies & Currents
17. .In the Day of His Power
18. Concluding Thoughts
19. The Strongholds of the Wilderness.
20. Amen
21. The Wilderness Journey

FORWARD

During the years of the 1960's there was a move of God which was often referred to as 'the charismatic movement!' It brought about a sweeping change among Christians who were suddenly energised with the fullness of the Holy Spirit and terms like ' born again!' and 'baptised in the Spirit' began to enter into the conversation of churches and of course Christians.

Established religion in the form of Anglican and even to some extent Catholic Christians were set as they had always been in forms of worship and service patterns that were the tradition and accepted way to worship God, in church! Services were printed in a book and to some extent the fact that you knew the words well enough, not to have to even look at the book; was in many ways that to attain! Surely these people were real Christians, they knew every word because they were there every week and said them every week, for years and years and years!

There was a hunger in people for more of God, more than what appeared to be the repeating of endless hollow words. Some people began to break away from the establishment into small groups where they eagerly sought to find a new way in God.

So was birthed the 'house group churches. They grew up with people who, came into a place where they **knew** that they were born again and they **knew** that they had been baptised in the Holy Spirit and they **knew** that their sin was forgiven. Worship was alive with joy and everything was Spirit led and Spirit infused. As with all that God brings among His people it was a time of great excitement and wonder. Alongside these new house group churches some came together and formed fellowship groups, often with links across the country. Many people were brought into the kingdom and even went out all over the world on missions carrying with them the blessings of new birth, Spirit led Christianity.

My Husband and I, were fortunate, as a couple to come into such a fellowship which had been birthed out of these beginnings. Stepping out of the deadness of established religion was an amazing and wonderful experience. These people believed exactly the same as the established Christians, except~

They actually, really believed!!

Faith alive, faith in action, a living reality that nothing else had ever demonstrated.

So over many years we had the blessing of growing and learning how to live and worship in a new and living way. It was a wonderful time knowing the freedom of waiting on the Holy Spirit. As time went on the fellowship that we belonged to actually purchased their own building. It was a retirement home that the council had closed and the church brought it for new home base.

There were alterations to the lay out and improvements made

until they ended up with a large meeting room, offices, catering spaces and residential accommodation. Two couples lived and worked full time in the building to run things and help with administration. It was a wonderful provision, not only for working in the local community but also for those coming back from mission work, who were able to have a place to stay and fellowship available.

This is the background to the situation that we as a married couple now found ourselves called to step into. We had both taken early retirement and had wanted to give of our time more into the work of God. So the stage was set and all that followed afterwards is recorded in these pages. It is a work of God prepared over many years and His leading it is, that we follow in all that we endeavour to do.

The outworking of this, never is as we expect! Our God moves in mysterious ways, past finding out! Never-the-less who would shy away from that wonderful blessing that comes from being in the will of God and giving of ourselves to His purposes? As for us there were years of plenty and years of great famine to follow, it is a pattern familiar to us all! However we can only follow that divine leading in the trust that our storehouses will have been sufficiently filled, while there was grain to be available! Never, ever, are we guaranteed an easy way. That was not the way that Jesus walked and it will not be ours either. We walk as He walked and face the hearts of men and women as He did, with all the vagaries of their changing opinions and actions

INTRODUCTION

The wilderness, a vast empty place where life struggles to survive. There is little to provide sustenance and certainly no place of comfort. Yet traditionally, the wilderness is the place where men through the ages have met with God and where God met with those that He chose and sent to do His will, to complete His purposes.

Is the wilderness experience still today the place where the Holy Spirit takes His people? We think of sand, dust and bitter winds and all are indeed pictures we associate with wilderness. But wilderness is really the place of emptiness, the absence of life. Here now faith is tested and easily lost; certainly the 'flim flam!' of ritual and reliance on religious systems quickly fails the weary traveller.

So many hopes and dreams, the reality of faith; what actually is it that we believe and know? Have we ever really experienced the true and living God, or is our life a cycle of church and reading words from books? In the wilderness, now it is all gone, perhaps even church itself and a loss as deep as death itself envelopes all.

Those who for whatever reason, find themselves walking in the place of wilderness, walk a lonely pathway and the endless nature of its emptiness becomes now the only constant. Sometimes the mind tries to compensate, travelling back to happier times, like looking through a porthole we see and remember the joy we had and yearn for that which we knew.

But it is gone and over and over again we are ushered back into the sand and the wind. He who leads into the wilderness of faith does not allow His servant to return until all that He has planned and foreseen is accomplished.

What then is the great and heavenly plan? Why would a loving wonderful God seem to take His own into this place of complete isolation and terrible despair? He is the Lord and the Almighty and all of time is in His hands. Only those of us in this mortal flesh are so consumed with the process of time and 'how long?'

He will wait and lead, taking us from the places in the world where we perhaps thought we were spiritual and even thought we were 'doing church!' and then, then He will open our eyes to Himself! In the wilderness there is only Him. It is the place where we learn to "lean on Him."

As we let go of all other things, or perhaps they are through life circumstances, taken away. So He comes to find us and lift us and to bring His sustaining presence. It is here in this place, that the true reality of our living Saviour becomes for each traveller; life and light and endless joy!

> "Who is this coming up from the wilderness,
> Leaning upon her beloved?"
> (Song of Solomon 8v5 NKJ)

Out of dust and loss; in distress and emptiness; somehow we find grace, we find a hand to touch upon and so we begin to learn and to understand the giving up of all that ever was, to Him. We learn to lean! We learn to open up ourselves in ways that perhaps we could never have previously known. Then we hear the 'Voice which is the sound of many waters!' as we wait upon Him, in the silent empty spaces.

He speaks into our barren dry hearts. Vision and purpose pours into those places which we had long despaired of anything but death and there in the dried up river bed life begins to come forth again and we find that we have not only a voice, but something to say!

But who is there to know these things? Who will ever hear? Now we are a voice in the wilderness and there is nowhere to speak and no-one to hear, or even know that we are there. He has taken our emptiness, healed our distresses lifted us up from the place of death.

What we now understand; all that is suddenly there within our heart; is the work of heavenly grace and it burns and glows with that eternal fire that fell on the altar for Elijah. He is the everlasting God and He has come to set a burning flame within our heart, now it glows with inextinguishable force. Speaking out from the wilderness place, brings with it the earnest assurance of having met with God. We cast our words out upon the winds that blow; releasing them into the great unknown. Now in the process of heavenly time, they may be available to others whose hearts

He has prepared. The voice in the wilderness, speaks from divine encounters worked upon a heart through the following of the solitary way.

> "I am the Lord, who made all things,
> who alone stretched out the heavens,
> who spread out the earth by myself,
> [25] who frustrates the signs of liars
> and makes fools of diviners,
> who turns wise men back
> and makes their knowledge foolish,
> [26] who confirms the word of his servant
> and fulfils the counsel of his messengers,"
>
> Isaiah 44 v 24 -26 (ESV)

> "I am God, and there is none like me,
> [10] declaring the end from the beginning
> and from ancient times things not yet done,
> saying, 'My counsel shall stand,
> and I will accomplish all my purpose,"
>
> Isaiah 46 v 10 (ESV)

A NEW WELL

"²⁴ And the Lord appeared to him the same night and said, "I am the God of Abraham your father. Fear not, for I am with you and will bless you and multiply your offspring for my servant Abraham's sake." ²⁵ So he built an altar there and called upon the name of the Lord and pitched his tent there. And there Isaac's servants dug a well."

Genesis 26 v 24-25 (ESV)

Sometimes there is a need for a new well. All that were a source of life before have for one reason or another become no longer able to provide. In this case they were argued over or had been stopped up by enemies. Eventually the servants of Isaac dug a well, found the new and living water, vital for their lives and settled in that place.

In the place where God spoke to him and made His presence known; Isaac made his settlement and those around him knew that this was a man whose life was blessed by God. The outworking of the presence of God in our lives must touch and register a difference to others who know Him not.

A question came to me one evening driving home after church. I had been listening to someone speak about how God had turned their life around after a prophetic word spoken about the digging of a new well. The illustration was quoted about how Isaac was led by God to dig a new well and the person had made a significant change in their life because of this verse of scripture.

As I drove home that night; with the words spoken still echoing through my head suddenly the question was turned towards me! "Would I be prepared to allow God to dig a new well in my life?" Phew! What on earth would that mean and how would it begin to happen? I stopped the car, so shocked I was, what seemed to me to be the voice of God suddenly pierced through all of my awareness. Even when I eventually arrived back home, I was stunned and left wondering what had really occurred?

At that time I was teaching full time, my husband though recently being made redundant now had a perfectly acceptable part time job. We had a lovely four bed detached and mainly things were progressing very normally. Our children were however now grown up and an empty nest brings with it thoughts of what next?

We chatter on so easily about 'having faith'! Oh it can sound very grand and how often we talk about trusting God in our lives; but really do we? Could we, could I trust in God to make very big changes in what my life was?

Now came the real questions; could I trust in God, in His presence and commitment to my life to actually make very definite changes?

There in the place where He is the very anchor and rock of everything? Could I let go of all that my life was and allow Him to begin to dig for me a new well? What would it mean and how could that happen? In following the will of God, there is and must surely be the attitude of letting go; the realisation of abandonment, and a sacrificial resignation to something perhaps beyond our expectation! The Israelites went out from Egypt into the desert where only the hand of God led them and provided for their needs.

In the well that God opens up, is all provision and blessing for our lives. But first He must be able to sink that well in us! He must and will cause His Spirit to form within our very depths; the well of God. The well of God is the experience from where we begin to know the living waters rising up and running free.

Rivers of Living Water

[37]On the last day of the feast, the great day, Jesus stood up and cried out, "If anyone thirsts, let him come to me and drink. [38]Whoever believes in me, as the Scripture has said, 'Out of his heart will flow rivers of living water.'"

John 7 v38 (ESV)

Many pieces fit together when the Holy Spirit moves upon our lives to call us into His purpose, there is a piece here and a piece from somewhere perhaps unexpected but one thing is certain; the calling of God keeps coming and coming. He does not leave us in doubt and uncertainty, **we know!**

His word, His leading and the steering of our way all begins to form the picture until we have before us the place of choice to move in obedience to that call, or to turn away. . The 'call' of God had come to us both, together and yet also separately. It never was or should be, "I think we should do this! Always the call of God is confirmed to all that He has purposed to begin in a new place. For us it was always joint and always parallel to our lives together before Him.

There was one particular weekend where there was a special weekend conference at our church. We wanted to go but because at that time we were living quite a long journey away it was going to entail a lot of car journeys. We thought we will ask if we can stay over at church for the weekend. This was agreed but then a situation arose where both the couples who lived in the church and looked after the arrangements, were unexpectedly both away for the weekend.

How amazing are the heavenly preparations, we often miss these divine promptings but their impact is never to be underestimated. Now we were asked to look after the building for the weekend and found ourselves plunged into the role that was to become our calling in God. As I have said these things are never "I think" or "Why don't we?" For both of us independently during that weekend we had the overriding feeling of being 'at home!' At that time neither of us spoke of it to the other, not wanting to prompt something. Yet both of us went home after that weekend with a clear and distinct calling etched into our hearts. It was not to go away nor dim in the days and weeks to come.

Looking back over many years in our lives there was a pattern of times and places, activities and situations where we saw and now recognised the preparing hand of God for us both. The opportunity came for early retirement and a way was suddenly now open which had not been there previously. When the hand of God is at work, suddenly mountains are removed and an open way becomes clear ahead of us.

Further to all of this there came an evening when we had gone to a business meeting at church. One of the couples who lived and worked at the church now suddenly announced to the church that they were leaving to move into their own home and retire from their duties. For many weeks previous to this we had become aware that God was calling us to go and live in at church becoming full time workers.

It was a great dilemma because for us we saw no way for that to be possible. As far as we knew there was no vacancy for a couple to move into the flat at church. God however knew exactly what was about to be required and in our hearts had prepared the way. As soon as they made their announcement, it all made sense, weeks and months of preparation now came together and we were ready.

There were many conversations to be had, prayer times and heart seeking before God to be really sure that we were following in His will and purposes. We both had confirmation that this was the will of God for us. It was a new well dug and prepared by heavenly hands and all of our previous life was cleared away.

So it was that in 2004 my husband and I moved out of our home and began a journey to begin working for our church as full time workers. We left our lovely four bed detached with newly completed conservatory to step into the unknown, even as we committed ourselves to do His will the house didn't sell, as we had expected it would.

There is that thought we are going to work for God so the house will just sell immediately!! Oh no! Not at all; it was a great test of faith to load up all of our things into a van and leave the house empty and waiting for someone to come along and buy it! He always takes us to the end of ourselves and the deep places that come out of that, are forever set as a place where the hand of God worked something in our lives. This is the building blocks of testimony, real truth experience in ordinary lives.

We knew that we were in His will and we knew the working out of His purposes for us. There were so many tests of faith, times when doors opened and we walked through. It was a wonderful time, filled with hope and promise.

On March 31st 2004 we first took over the flat. It was our decision to delay our actual moving in until we had decorated through and prepared everything ready for the next stage of our lives before God to fully begin. When we initially walked into the flat, on the first day we were able to visit; looking out through the kitchen windows we saw that the trees outside were full and heavy with beautiful pink blossom. It seemed to be a sign of all that God had for us in the richness of His provision for those who are in His charge. For both of us we had answered the 'call' and everything of our lives and our substance, we brought into that place of service for Him

Eventually we made the transition and moved into the flat in June of 2004. It was a wonderful and exciting time. Many people had helped us to decorate and even before we moved in there was a sense of something new for the church and a coming together of people to bring of their help and expertise.

Our lives were full and busy and yet it seemed but a small thing for the joy of serving Him and for being available to our church and the people around us. With great energy we had decorated all of the flat, wanting to make it light and bright for those who would come through our door, and many, many did! No day was ever the same, people came from every situation, needing comfort or help or just a cup of tea and a chat. It was the calling of our hearts to be available to all and we gave in a place of great joy. The door was always open and we were always available!

For us the church and its people were all important and in every way we sought to bring blessing and care to those who came to our door. We gave of ourselves, our substance and poured ourselves out because He, our Lord Jesus Christ; had so done for us. It was a pattern set, a way prepared.

We had had no training for what we found ourselves suddenly placed into, working with the homeless and people on drugs, anyone who came to the church! But God, who is rich in mercy was our guide, our help and our resource. We constantly needed to turn to Him for that help and support required for frequently very difficult places and situations, where we seemed to be out of our depth.

Sometimes it was a plate of sandwiches or a hot drink, always with lots of sugar! Then there were those who needed support and a shoulder to lean on. People of every walk of life appeared at the door of our flat at all times of the day, endlessly! We tried to encourage those who lived alone in the church to join us for meals and other special occasions. After the morning meeting on Sundays often their were up to fourteen or more, people around our dining room table, it was a work of art preparing and timing a meal which would be easily shared and ready very quickly!

There was so much joy shared at that table and so many lonely people who were able to find a hot meal and company. Fellowship is a word we use very easily, it is one of the most important aspects of our lives and ministry to each other within the church. So often we attend church and go home forgetting that there are those who are alone, and have a desperate need for company. They so easily fall between the cracks and with all of our good intentions are left feeling on the outside, mainly people need to have a part and a place, these are the vital inclusions we must never forget.

THE PLACE OF VISION

So it was that our new well was firmly established and for both of us there was an endless schedule of people and meetings, the whole spectrum of church life continually revolving around us. This was indeed a time of great joy and blessing and it was all of our heart to serve and be available in every way that we could.

As we became more settled into our lives serving the church we began to see that, where there had once been a vibrant free running ministry of the Holy Spirit, now it had become a quieter more sedate existence where things were generally planned out. Much of the patterns of our worship remained as they had always been but increasingly planning became more and more evident. Gone was the Spirit led and Spirit filled wonder which had been our previous experience. It's amazing how you never see it happening but we had become an 'old church' settling for something less. It was on our hearts that there was a need for a time of refreshing, a further touch of the life of God.

At this time I had little concept of revival and had never really read about it or given the subject any focussed study. However, through our living in the church and the work we were involved with; more and more we became aware of the need for a new place of blessing and the wonder that renewal brings into the life of church. We were in a church which had for many years known the riches of the moving of the Holy Spirit, but even so, very slowly a tiredness creeps in, we slip into something less and have not even noticed.

One day I was walking along a corridor in the church building, I can see it now as if it had just this moment happened. A very ordinary day just doing very normal things. How amazing it is that when the Holy Spirit chooses to open to us a window in heaven, always we are caught unawares. Then it is that what was the very ordinary becomes bathed in heavenly light and will never ever be either the same again nor will it fade from our memory. I did not instigate it. Nor did I realise that it was to bring about a seismic shift in my thinking about church and how we go about our **'doing of church.'**

There came to me at this moment a sudden opening up of, the first, of a series of scriptures. It was as though a great light shone and I both saw and understood in a new way. I was taken up into the heavenlies and the light of the Glory of God transformed my life for ever. I stood still in the corridor and it seemed that everything around me became distant, while my heart and mind were flooded with the piercing light of heaven.

Further to that, it happened again, over the next few days four passages of scripture were opened up to my understanding in a deep incisive way. Each piece of scripture came again as a direct intervention of the Holy Spirit. Now they came together as a pattern which flowed on, one from the other; each extending the vision until it became a whole and complete picture, given by the Spirit.

The Lord initiated this place within my heart for Himself and it seemed to me as though heaven itself had opened up, revealing truth, bringing direction and purpose. It brought to me a vision of revival and as it were, a heavenly plan for God's intervention in our lives as His church.

Also it brought me into a new and deeper experience of prayer, a place I had not known before. I was drawn now into a deep experience of intercession for the church. It was the longing of my heart that this promise brought through heavenly vision would be fulfilled. It was truly my deepest desire for His blessing to be released once more and a new outpouring of the fullness of the Holy Spirit for those, who were our family in Christ.

Mainly it was the custom in our church group for people to share a word of encouragement or testimony during the Sunday morning gatherings. This seemed to be an obvious move, at some point I would share with the church what the Lord had revealed to me. Surely this was the right and normal thing to do? Nevertheless I was somehow held back from doing that. I have no idea way but I found myself making an arrangement with God with regard to what He had revealed to me.

So it was that I entered into a tryst with God. The word to which he had opened now to me, I would not share in any way with the church until I knew the moving of His Holy Spirit to do so. All had to be of God and nothing of my planning or arranging. It was His place of vision and only God was to unlock that for the church in His time.

This was now the beginning of finding for myself a deep and meaningful experience of intercession, far beyond anything I had ever previously experienced. He called me into the place of prayer and there I stayed for a very long time. Actually I waited four years before the Lord opened up for me the moment to share the vision which He had planted within my heart. Why you may wonder was it necessary for that amount of time to pass? It was very necessary because during that time I was soaked and immersed into the vision, it became a living part of my very breath.

We found a few people who shared our longing for a revival of new life in our church. Even the leadership shunned our aspirations and had become content in what they had; the tragedy of so much complacency; when all of the blessings of heaven are available to those who are His. Eventually about six of us began to pray and we prayed and we prayed for days and weeks and years! There was such a yearning and seeking for that blessing to come, but always we met with so much opposition.

There came a day when during a Sunday morning meeting I knew that this was the time and now God moved within my heart to share the fullness of the vision to which He had immersed my heart into. After asking permission to share I gave the whole picture of the vision given to me by the Holy Spirit. Some there were who responded and were genuinely moved. However it was very interesting that from the church leadership I was blasted, yes blasted not for giving a word in the Spirit. Rather because it took over too much of their prepared time!!

After not a small argument, I stood my ground and asked "Was it correct for me to obey the leading of the Holy Spirit, or worry about their prepared plan?" Sometime much later, that particular leader wanted to know what I actually shared. "I didn't listen to anything you said" he told me because it was not your time to speak! I replied that I was very sorry but the time was now gone and it would not be repeated.

How it is that we become easily comfortable with our state? The way things were gives way to formalisation and acceptance of something less! Our searching and looking for that which was new did not meet with people who wanted to get up and go after more;

rather it was looked upon as being a bit 'odd' or rather tiresome! It is my understanding that our Heavenly Father is always ready to bless and nurture His people and His church; always wanting to move us on and bring fresh new places where His Holy Spirit moves and breathes into us the living waters of hope and joy.

But it is as in all of His dealings with His people that we must constantly seek His will and be obedient to the speaking of God in our midst. Without the desire to move and to listen and change the church becomes stale and the vibrancy of our life, as church slips away into the grey mist. Never-the-less it is also important to remember, that while the Holy Spirit comes again and again during seasons of renewal, bringing a wind of change to lift and renew life that has stagnated. There is never in any way a removal of the basic ground of holiness and the dealing with sin. Attitudes relative to social and modern thinking do not necessarily reflect nor come alongside that which is the plum line of God!

So it was in those days, that the vision which had filled my heart and become my source of direction was not met with enthusiasm and God does not force upon us even blessing if we turn our hearts away and decide on another pathway. There was no revival and no new infilling of life and eventually the will for people to pray seemed to ebb away! It was a terrible loss and disappointment but again I could only submit to the will and the purpose of God. His is the life and the vision beyond our limited grasp; we see but dimly, He alone knows all things and their working.

Regardless of all, as the years have passed what I now call 'the place of vision' became for me, a marker in my heart, it is the ground from which I have been drawn deeper and deeper into prayer and the seeking of His purposes for His glory to be revealed upon us as His church, through us as His people.

During these days I found a new depth of prayer. It was truly a closet place where time stood still and entering into His presence the Holy Spirit nurtured the speaking of God and enlarged vision within my heart. Now I found something of the reality of prayer; of waiting on Him, with nothing else to distract. How little we really know and ever really touch upon real prayer; prayer that opens heaven and moves the mountains of impossibility around us. This was what I now called **'the place of prayer'**. It is the meeting with God, where heaven is open and we are drawn into its reality and purpose. Here is the opportunity to 'listen' to the 'heartbeat of heaven' and be drawn deeper and deeper into the **'Beautiful Presence'**!

What most Christians experience as prayer in our churches today is a poor and lifeless activity, mainly reading words that others have written down, or prepared earlier! Prayer should be passion! It must come from a longing heart, where the Spirit has worked, bringing forth words of power and hope eternal.

Prayer should speak the voice of heaven and even command the 'wind and the waves'! One thing I know, that those things planted into our hearts by the Holy Spirit; do not fade nor do they lose the urgency of those moments of revelation. Rather they grow and mature, becoming within us a deep and passionate longing, a waiting for the time when heaven shall be opened and all the joy of His purpose, fulfilled most wonderfully.

Many things that I was deeply praying and seeking for in those days, still today remain unfulfilled and the endless mystery of prayer and the outworking of all that we have longed and hoped for ever continues. Brave is the soul who claims to have found the secret of answered prayer and perhaps even a system or mechanism of how that works!

It is however my own continuing testimony that sometimes it is not the answers to our prayers which bring about real and lasting change. I have found rather it is the wonder, of entering into the Heavenly Presence, to become drawn and ever drawn into the arms of our Heavenly Father. We become now taken up with the experience of the 'Heavenly embrace' so much that all other things which had seemed so very important, now slip away. We look upon the Lord of Glory and are ourselves forever changed.

Oh yes, we need to know that our prayers are answered and the Eternal response is always available as we come to seek His hand. It is however not in our limited vision to know and fully understand the ways of our God. I most firmly do however believe that there is what can only be best describes as a 'heavenly bank', here it is that every prayer and our constant longings before His throne await that perfect eternal release in heavenly time.

For myself as I continued to find something of understanding with those things which now filled up my heart and soul constantly, it is perhaps a journey where understanding and the yearnings of heaven become entwined. In the beginning there is the innocent, which expects it to be today or tomorrow! The passing of time brings maturity to the vision and begins to work the process of abandonment where all must become Him and we are just a conduit, a vessel from which He is able to speak and work.

I now know that my expectation for blessing and new move of God where I was then, in the church I loved, was a normal response. These people were to me 'bone of my bone and flesh of my flesh' I could see no further than the hope of blessing for my church and my family in God. But there is so much more and now, I am looking at church upon a vastly wider horizon.

Those things He has needed to work through circumstances and situations where the cross of Christ has made deep and expansive cuts into the fabric of my life. These are never easy and the cost, beyond any words to express. Will we, would we, pay this great price to see the church become again alive and fresh where the rivers of living water flow with heavenly abandonment? The scriptures, that came to me, familiar to us all, are used so often to speak about new life and revival.

However, I now saw them, not in isolation but as a part of a pattern in which the church becomes again alive and renewed, invigorated, to become both relevant and active for a new generation of His power working. This process of revival must bring first the church into a new place of life, then follows increase as the lost are brought into salvation. The cross of Jesus Christ and the name of Jesus Christ must become again the powerful driving force, it is; the way to life, it is the working mechanism of that life, to every born again believer.

Without the cross there is only a poor copy of life, ritual and empty words repeated over and over because they perhaps appear to be spiritual. It is a deep meeting with the living Christ and the work of the cross that brings about transforming life, touched by His redeeming love. The revealing of sin in the lives of men and women is a messy process that takes no account of protocol and gentle restful Christianity. The death of Christ, how can that be ever anything but a bloody and a great horror! 'There is power, wonder working power, in His precious blood' at the foot of the cross where there is only ourselves and Him.

These now are the scriptures that came to me as a place of vision, a place of renewal where His life again flows and there is an abundance of both grace and mercy poured out. In every way I wanted it to be for my, church, where we were; but they did not want it and now still I hold the vision and wait for heaven to bring fulfilment to that which has been spoken, for surely it cannot return to Him void and perhaps somewhere at some time there will be a group of people who are willing to seek after Him for the opening of the doors of heaven and glory to be released upon their church and community.

Always it is so, that when we are prepared to meet those requirements that He has set down for us in His Word; then the windows of heaven will be opened and he will indeed rain down upon us righteousness, fullness and grace like a flood.

SCRIPTURE (1)

During this time my bible was New King James version and all of the scriptures related to this period of the leading of God I have therefore left in that version. Please forgive any confusion with regard to that issue, the words here represent many hours of soaking before God and praying His words out during my times of waiting upon Him.

The Dry Bones Live

"The hand of the LORD came upon me and brought me out in the Spirit of the LORD, and set me down in the midst of the valley; and it was full of bones. ²Then He caused me to pass by them all around, and behold, there were very many in the open valley; and indeed they were very dry. ³And He said to me, "Son of man, can these bones live?" So I answered, "O Lord GOD, You know."

Ezekiel 37 New King James Version (NKJV)

Here is the place of beginning. He comes to take us out of everything that our lives have ever been. It is His will to come and take us from what we know and is, so often our comfort zone, into a place which is of His will and His choosing. He comes in the place of revival to restore that which is dry and worn out, where we have lost vitality and all that speaks of abundant fullness in the flowing of the Holy Spirit.

> " Again He said to me, "Prophesy to these bones, and say to them, 'O dry bones, hear the word of the LORD! [5] Thus says the Lord GOD to these bones: "Surely I will cause breath to enter into you, and you shall live. [6] I will put sinews on you and bring flesh upon you, cover you with skin and put breath in you; and you shall live. Then you shall know that I am the LORD..."
> Ezekiel 37 New King James Version (NKJV)

The Lord is speaking of His life and His vitality becoming our living experience and understanding. Always it is His purpose, **'that we shall know He is the Lord'**.

> "Also He said to me, "Prophesy to the breath, prophesy, son of man, and say to the breath,
> 'Thus says the Lord GOD: "Come from the four winds, O breath, and breathe on these slain, that they may live." ' " [10] So I prophesied as He commanded me, and breath came into them, and they lived, and stood upon their feet, an exceedingly great army. Ezekiel 37 New King James Version (NKJV)"

"**Come from the four winds O breathe...**" Here for me became the source of prayer, the longing heart crying out, Oh come, Oh breathe; breath of God come. It is the constant place of waiting and watching for 'the cloud as small as a man's hand', the rustling in the tree tops.

Prayer that consumes, prayer that becomes a place rooted and grounded; it will not go away nor will it listen to the many voices that cry out "ridiculous and impossible!" Prayer that survives the earthquake and the storms; the terrible desert winds, it rises again when one thought it was long dead and lost, to cry out to heaven, to touch again upon the 'throne'.

> "[11] Then He said to me, "Son of man, these bones are the whole house of Israel. They indeed say, 'Our bones are dry, our hope is lost, and we ourselves are cut off!' [12] Therefore prophesy and say to them, 'Thus says the Lord God: "Behold, O My people, I will open your graves and cause you to come up from your graves, and bring you into the land of Israel. [13] Then you shall know that I am the Lord, when I have opened your graves, O My people, and brought you up from your graves. [14] I will put My Spirit in you, and you shall live, and I will place you in your own land. Then you shall know that I, the Lord, have spoken it and performed it," says the Lord."
>
> **Ezekiel 37 New King James Version (NKJV)**

We will only know Him as Lord, when we have opened ourselves up, to allow Him full and complete access to all of our lives. So often there is a partial opening up to God, perhaps at conversion, but can we go on from that place? Dare we allow ourselves to be vulnerable and exposed in truly a deep and searching way? Perhaps we have been 'in the church!' a Christian for many years, is there still more in God yet undiscovered?

What is possible, that is as yet unrealised and are we prepared to pay the price? Oh so often that price will hold us back, loss of face, to become unravelled before those who thought us to be so spiritual!

What does it mean for Him to open up our graves?

Why is the church so often dry and lost? Ritual has taken the place of the Spiritual and acceptance of this brings so much death to so many in the church today. When He comes to open up our graves, 'the all' of our lives is laid before Him. There is no hiding, no excuses. All that we are, everything; all that has been pushed down perhaps for years, now open ~ upon the altar laid out before the searching gaze of heaven. It is a terrible and terrifying place! Always there will be massive opposition to this, even those we thought to be so very spiritual, most often are the voice of reason!

But, when the sword of truth is allowed free reign in our lives; like the grapes that must be pruned with such relentless vigour for a good harvest, so with us ~ the knife that cuts away the dead wood, also brings the possibility of new life ~ abundant life. That heavenly knife, which cuts through everything with such relentless power is the cross of Christ. Where the cross had had free working in our lives, the deeper the cut ~ the more blessing ~ the more fruit ~ the more joy ~ the more of God's Holy Spirit released within our lives.

He comes to open up our graves so that a new way can be established, a new place begun and the cross of Christ can work fully and deeply bringing us into the amazing and wonderful knowledge that HE IS LORD!

It is impossible to know the 'joy of the Lord' unless we have been at the foot of the cross!

It is impossible to live the Christian life in fullness and vitality unless we have allowed Him to open up our graves!

That huge stone which kept everything down and hidden from sight, must go. It must be Divinely lifted up; then the very breath of heaven is ours and freedom, unspeakable joy, power from on high become the very circulating force of our lives. Life full and free, amazing grace, amazing and wonderful release.

Now we are ready to work within the church and for the church, to turn our gaze outwards to those who know Him not! It is my belief that true revival can only come when the Holy Spirit falls upon His people to reveal Jesus Christ in His risen glory. When that happens we can only fall on our faces ~ there is nothing more. It is and must be entirely the work of God moving by and through His Holy Spirit upon His people; the church. Why do we not yearn and look for it to be so? Why as we satisfied with so little in our churches every Sunday?

SCRIPTURE (2)

The Good News of Salvation

**61 "The Spirit of the Lord GOD is upon Me,
Because the LORD has anointed Me
To preach good tidings to the poor;**

**He has sent Me to heal the broken-hearted,
To proclaim liberty to the captives,
And the opening of the prison to those who are bound;
² To proclaim the acceptable year of the LORD,
And the day of vengeance of our God;
To comfort all who mourn,**

**³ To console those who mourn in Zion,
To give them beauty for ashes,
The oil of joy for mourning,
The garment of praise for the spirit of heaviness;
That they may be called trees of righteousness,
The planting of the LORD, that He may be glorified."**

Isaiah 61 v1-3 NKJ)

First He comes to renew the church and prepare 'the army of God' to do battle for the souls of the lost. Now in this passage He speaks to us of what church is and should be.

The Spirit of the Lord is upon me ~ now becomes **US** ~ the church

The Spirit of the Lord ~ **IS UPON US!**

- **We are to preach the good tidings...**
- **We are to heal the broken hearted...**
- **We are to proclaim liberty to the captives...**

This passage which Jesus Christ read out and claimed for himself at the start of His ministry must continue through, to now speak for the church of Jesus Christ.

- **We are!!!**
- **We are!!!**
- **We are His church,**
- **His voice,**
- **His body,**
- **His Life to others.**
- **We are** ~ this is a mission statement for every church and as it continues through, it speaks of those things which should be the normal expression of the work of Christ through His Spirit in every church.

The Spirit of the Lord of Glory rests upon us as HIS church!

This is the work and ministry of Jesus Christ and in turn it is the work and ministry of His church.

It is my heart longing and belief; that the Lord's purpose is to come to us as His church. To revive us and flood us with His power and His joy and His fullness of life so that we may be effective as His church in our generation. That He may be glorified in His church through His people.

SCRIPTURE (3)

The Parable of the Sower

"[4] And when a great multitude had gathered, and they had come to Him from every city, He spoke by a parable: [5] "A sower went out to sow his seed. And as he sowed, some fell by the wayside; and it was trampled down, and the birds of the air devoured it. [6] Some fell on rock; and as soon as it sprang up, it withered away because it lacked moisture. [7] And some fell among thorns, and the thorns sprang up with it and choked it.

[8] But others fell on good ground, sprang up, and yielded a crop a hundredfold." When He had said these things He cried, "He who has ears to hear, let him hear!"

The Purpose of Parables

[9] Then His disciples asked Him, saying, "What does this parable mean?"

[10] And He said, "To you it has been given to know the mysteries of the kingdom of God . . ."

Luke 8 New King James Version (NKJV)

Everything builds. This is now the directive to the church. First comes renewal ~ then purpose and directive ~ now going out to do. As church we are commissioned to be those who go out to sow; the seed being the word of God, the growth resulting comes from that work of sowing.

So many different places the seed falls and with corresponding different outcomes but still we must keep sowing because that seed which falls on the good ground will bring forth the growth and the extension of the kingdom of God. We cannot make judgements about where we sow and what type of ground it appears to fall upon. Only He brings the life, it is for us to keep on sowing in faith.

SCRIPTURE (4)

". . .⁴When He had stopped speaking, He said to Simon, "Launch out into the deep and let down your nets for a catch."
⁵But Simon answered and said to Him, "Master, we have toiled all night and caught nothing; nevertheless at Your word I will let down the net."

Luke 5 New King James Version (NKJ)

As we go out to sow the seed, we are often called to launch out into hard places; deeper waters, where perhaps we have toiled much in the past for little reward. Many will say "We have been here before, done this before and all for nothing!" If He is directing us as His church we must sow the seed where He leads us to sow; to let down our nets at His word.

"⁶And when they had done this, they caught a great number of fish, and their net was breaking. ⁷So they signalled to their partners in the other boat to come and help them. And they came and filled both the boats, so that they began to sink.
⁸When Simon Peter saw it, he fell down at Jesus' knees, saying, "Depart from me, for I am a sinful man, O Lord!"

Luke 5 New King James Version (NKJ)

In this place of vision which the Holy Spirit opened up to me, here was the final touch of His grace and the bringing together of everything in order that others may come to find salvation and that revival might again renew the church. As we are renewed, as we accept our direction as church and begin to move out sowing seed perhaps in places that we have not previously known any growth; so now most gloriously does He come to fill those nets which we let down in the hard places around our churches.

Perhaps we will be astonished at the catch of fish that will be ours! So much so that others will need to come alongside to help to process them. When revival comes the natural barriers fall away and we are together responsible for the harvest of wonder that our nets have revealed

Over our years as we served and lived in the flat at our beloved church this was the continuing marker upon my heart for not only our revival as a single local church but also as a wider impacting of the moving of the Holy Spirit upon church around us. As I have said it became for me a continuing platform to seek for the fulfilment of a heavenly vision. Prayer became alive and entering my closet place day after day I called out to God for His blessings to fall upon us.

It was also very evident, as I have previously mentioned that a new seeking for a further experience of blessing, was not eagerly received by those around us. One of the most memorable and telling conversations we had during those days resulted in a comment from a prominent church member when talking about a new move of God. His words came cutting through my heart like a great sword, sharp and ruthless as he very glibly said, "Been there done that, got the Tshirt!" He turned and walked away with no interest in our conversation or any heart to seek after God in prayer for our church.

The words have never left me and paint a desperate picture of how we so easily slip away from life and grace, because we think that once long ago we opened up our lives to God so now we have nothing further to do. Walking with God is never a once only entrance and then we coast along because we brought a ticket long ago! Yet for many Christians it is exactly that, we have arrived, we go to church, what more could there be?

Is it conceivable that the Spirit of God only ever wishes to work in our lives on a 'one off' basis? Life by its own definition must be new and thriving, fresh and now active for this moment today! We cannot live as Christians on yesterday's blessings and yesterday's bread. That as we well know was never in the plan of God for His people! Yesterday's bread grew worms and stank, perhaps we need to think about that more in our churches.

THE WATERFALL OF GRACE

Much time had now passed since first, I saw in my heart the vision for a revival, in the moving of the Holy Spirit through our church people. It became for me an all-consuming passion and prayer developed into a new and living place; where yearning and seeking and 'seeing the vision' was now embedded in the daily routine of life.

Every day I went to meet with God in a little corner of the church which became to me a small corner of heaven. In that time I entered into His presence and prayed my heart out for blessing upon the church where we were. Wonderful it was, time stood still and the Holy Spirit moved upon my heart. This is where I actually learned to pray. Meeting with God day by day, entering into a heart experience of crying out for the windows of heaven to open, for the winds of the Holy Spirit to be released.' Blow wind of God, 'come from the four corners of the Earth', as written in Ezekiel, this became my heart longing and expectation.

Months passed into years, time it seemed was suspended. I held out my hand to heaven and waited and watched, but few around me either wanted the vision or had any expectation of it. The fulfilment of the vision would bring change and change was an activity that was not particularly looked for, or wanted!

Great walls of organisation appeared, where previously there had been an open Spirit led life. They had become so much a part of the life of church that no-one really saw the process of them; indifference and complacency, the establishment of tradition and order where once flowed the rivers of life. How it is that we block His way with our ordering and establishing and setting down of patterns? **"This is the way we do things!" "We have planned this now for today's service!"** As soon as you hear this, the way of the Spirit has been blocked.

I saw in my heart that He had prepared for the church, 'a waterfall of grace' .It was the experience where all was swept aside as the Holy Spirit flowed freely and abundantly. One morning, waiting upon God, these words came to me flowing in the Holy Spirit. As I waited in His presence, now the words flowed upon my heart and I was filled with the wonder of God.

The Waterfall of Grace ~ A Gift of God

The waterfall of grace is the walls of Jericho fallen down
The shout of God heard in the camp!

Do you not hear in your heart, the sound of the water?
It rushes over stones and boulders;
Pours down with immeasurable power?

That which He has released,
Flows with an unstoppable force,

It is grace poured forth ~
It is life to the dead.
The recovery of sight to the blind ~
And hearing to the deaf.

For those who are weary,
Stumbling with uncertain steps,
He comes to lift them to safety,
Onto the highway of life

He comes to restore,
To renew ~ to revive
And to set in place the church ~
His church
Ready for the work and the purposes of His heart.

As with a mighty torrent of water ~
That cascades into deep and empty places,
There is a mist,
Which rises up ~
Forming a haze of vapour,

So in the moving of God
There would be as it were ~
A cloud spreading out.
All around it would reach
Bringing momentum ~
To the stirrings of the hand of God.

It will be the extension of His grace
To those who are around,
For His church ~
His people.

This is the cloud of His Holy Presence,
Therefore as the cloud,
In bible times ~
Covered the mountain of God,

So it will extend downwards,
Across the lives of men and women.
A holy and extending presence
Bring good news,
The hope of salvation,
To those who are lost.

He requires of us, that we stand,
Focussed to maintain the place of faith.
Ready for His perfect will.
Abandoned to Him alone!

The waterfall of grace,
Pours freely,
With mercy and power it is spontaneously given.
Are we ready to receive its mighty flow?
Will we indeed,
Abandon all of our preconceptions?
Church and faith,
Our planned routines?

To wait upon Him ~
To receive of Him.

The waterfall of grace,
Passes through our planned procedure.
He works in ways beyond our expectation,
The Holy Presence is given ~
To those who will receive.

The shout of God is heard in the camp,
The horn of salvation is blown.
Will we ~

Can we respond to the call?

The waterfall of grace is now released,
Mighty torrents flowing ~
The river of God continues onwards,
For you and for me ~
For His church to be renewed once more.

HEAVENLY ENCOUNTER

To my knowledge,
I have never seen an angel.
Nor had the fortune of any such encounter.
However ~
That is not to state,
That no such miracle has been,
Mysteriously gifted upon my life.

Blind and shielded vision ~
Is ours,
So often we only see,
As through a glass darkly.
While heavenly encounters ~
Move freely among us.
Invisible and yet seen!
As we so often,
Lack the discernment,
To actually perceive.

"Now when Herod was about to bring him out, on that very night, Peter was sleeping between two soldiers, bound with two chains, and sentries before the door were guarding the prison. ⁷And behold, an angel of the Lord stood next to him, and a light shone in the cell. He struck Peter on the side and woke him, saying, "Get up quickly."

Acts 7 v 6-7 (ESV)

There are those times,
When suddenly in our darkest moment,
A light will shine.
Breaking through ~
The impenetrable and unrelenting blackness.

Suddenly ~
The Light of Heaven,
Breaks through.
Light filling and streaming everywhere.
A heavenly encounter opens up.

We shield our eyes,
The glorious brightness,
Powerfully impacting our senses.
Time it seems has stopped.
We are most wonderfully ~
Lifted into glory!

"He thought he saw a vision",
Doors previously locked,
Bars of impenetrable resolve,
Now spontaneously opened.
All resistance terminated,
An open way secured.

"⁸ The wind blows where it wishes, and you hear its sound, but you do not know where it comes from or where it goes. So it is with everyone who is born of the Spirit."
John 3 v8 (ESV)

The wind blows where it will,
We do not know,
Where it came from,
Or where it will go.
It is born of the Holy Spirit,
Invisible glory,
Moving across the lives of men and women.

He sends His angels,
To speak words of prophecy ~
To warn of impending disaster ~
To open the prison doors.

Heavenly encounters ~
Carried upon heavenly purpose,
Wonderful, glorious glimpses into heaven.
Building His church.

We speak, that which we know,
Bear witness of that we have seen and heard,
These are heavenly portals opened,
Gloriously woven across our way.

The man spoke to Peter,
Arise ~ get up quickly.
There is a need,
To be obedient to the heavenly vision,
Following the leading now given.

"**[13] At midday, O king, I saw on the way a light from heaven, brighter than the sun that shone around me and those who journeyed with me.**
"**[14] And when we had all fallen to the ground, I heard a voice saying to me in the Hebrew language, 'Saul, Saul, why are you persecuting me? It is hard for you to kick against the goads.'**
[15] And I said, 'Who are you, Lord?' And the Lord said, 'I am Jesus whom you are persecuting.
Acts 26 v12-15 (ESV)

In these unearthly moments,
When the mysteries of heaven are wonderfully opened,
We are suddenly afraid.
This is a heavenly encounter.
We are in our earth bound restrictions,
Overcome with fear.

The angelic vision is sent,
Through the favour of God.
We find His favour ~
It is released across our lives.
Bringing news of happiness,
The joy of the Lord.

"And the LORD answered me:
"Write the vision;
make it plain on tablets,
so he may run who reads it.
³ For still the vision awaits its appointed time;
it hastens to the end—it will not lie.
If it seems slow, wait for it;
it will surely come; it will not delay."
Habakkuk 2 v 203 (ESV)

The vision is yet for an appointed time.
Though it seems to us,
That it is delayed,
Even thwarted,
It cannot be.

The King of Glory,
Has sent His angel.
To open impossible doors,
Speaking of glorious matters.
It will surely come.

Oh Lord,
By Your gracious hand,
The scriptures were opened.
Expanded vision ~
Illuminated pages to be understood.
Eternal possibilities revealed.
The light of heaven,
Filling a heart with wonder.

Now a very ordinary day,
Is transformed forever,
Becoming gloriously wonderful.
Your hand revealed,
The Living Word spoken,
With burning fire,
Into an ordinary life.

These words will never fade,
Nor will they become forgotten.
As all things must wait ~
For heaven's appointed time.
So the vision awaits,
For the day of the Lord's power.

All must be fulfilled,
Expectantly we wait.
These are the touches of His purpose,
The favour of God,
Empowering our lives.

We are taken,

Into heavenly places,

Far beyond our restricted vision.

Now He opens our eyes, our ears ~

To reveal His will and purpose.

WRITE THE VISION

Write the vision,
Make it plain.
Clear and transparent,
For all who would wish to know.

Only for a moment ~
The heavenly portal opened.
Light piercing through,
An open way,
Given gloriously.

Here is truth,
The beauty of heaven.
Now expanded,
Like the clouds parting on a gloomy day ~
Sunlight comes flooding through.

Write the vision,
These moments are to be held,
All that we saw ~
Safely kept.
Until all of time has been fulfilled.

We hold the words,
The vision deeply imprinted,
Now a part of us ~
It has become.
For an appointed time,

There is no delay ~
Regardless of those who refuse,
Turning their backs,
Upon this golden moment.

The eternal tide ~
Is never blocked.
Always eventually ~
The righteous will of God,
Will be established.

Only know ~ be assured,
It will not delay ~
Never can this heavenly purpose
Return to Him void

THE DARK JOURNEY

The dark journey is a place where knowing the vision of God for the revival of His church, there came for me, a setting off on a pilgrimage to find a further knowing of Him. It was a searching and seeking for fire upon the altar; where all that was laid down in prayer and seeking for the fulfilling of His word brought a new requirement in the walk of faith. The dark journey was a leap of faith beyond any I had yet known. How could one make the choice to leave behind so much to enter to willingly into a terrible darkness?

I came to realise that I needed an anointing of the Holy Spirit beyond anything that I had previously experienced. I needed Him to take me beyond myself, beyond who I was or what I was within the church; into the all-consuming fire of God. Deeper and yet deeper; further and yet further to be lost in Him and abandoned to His hand.

> "Come Holy Ghost my soul inspire
> And light me with celestial fire.
> Thou the anointing Spirit art
> Who dost Thy sevenfold gifts impart.
>
> Thy blessed unction from above
> Is comfort, life and fire of love,
> Enable with perpetual light
> The dullness of our blinded sight"
> (John Cosin 1594-1672)

These words of the very old hymn, became to me an anchor a place where I was held as daily my heart pleaded for the blessing of God to be given upon our church. Day after day they echoed through my mind and my worship times. Come Holy Ghost, yes oh come and inspire my heart with fire from off the altar of God?

Obedience is a not a popular word in the church today, but it is the absolute requirement in the walking of every believer. This time now chronicled is what can only be called 'a dark journey' of the soul. In these years, I was finding my way to be established into a deeper experience of the living presence of God. There had been passages of time that were very difficult in former days when I was first seeking to find salvation. However this experience now related was so much deeper and searching than I had previously known.

The relating of this period of time, covers the days, weeks, months and years now spent in the wilderness of darkness, while only the hand of God could lead and where all else was lost from view. On the 5-9-09 I have recorded that this was the moment when the dark journey began. I entered into it willingly and obediently, believing entirely it to be all that was the will and the purpose of God for me. He had come to make a deep cut across my life with the 'sword of truth' and to bring the cross into the deeper and yet untouched places in my life.

I knew not where He was taking me or for what purpose. I just followed the leading of God in faith. In my heart everything was laid down and given for the securing of that to which I had seen before the throne of grace, for a revival in the life of our church and the surrounding area where we were.

In the scriptures that had come to me, which I have called the 'place of vision' were the words where in Ezekiel, God says that He must open up our graves in order for us to fully 'know' that He is the Lord.

Now at this time a word was prophesied over me in a time of prayer. It said that there was a place deep within my life and locked away that God had never been given free access to and I was challenged to open myself up to God in a further way than I had yet known.

I had no knowledge of this hidden place, nor was I in any way deliberately hiding anything from God. Actually, rather I can now say that the Holy Spirit saw what I did not and knew, that to which I had no awareness of at all. The Lord now led me into a dark and awful place and little did I know that it would become much darker and bring my entire walk of faith into complete devastation. We should always beware of our limited horizons, we never, ever see clearly and we always underestimate the absolute perfection of the working hand of God.

When I entered this very dark place I actually thought it would be for a short time! I really expected that it would be a catalyst for blessing for my church! Oh dear, Oh dear how very wrong I was and the working out of its fullness was a process of terrible despair beyond anything I could ever have seen.

Would I have entered into this dark place had I seen fully where it led to? Very difficult to be honest and say of course! Sometimes our restricted vision is a safer place to stand, it saves us from those effects which we would not cope with seeing. Also it saves us from the rash unguarded statements of faith, which in its self is a blessing! As it was this journey that I now set out upon was to last for many years and the travelling affected both of us, becoming a great and terrible nightmare.

For my husband and I what had begun with so much promise in our living and working for the church began to change. Attitudes and agendas within the church began to affect us and our place became more and more difficult. For both of us, the vision of revival we had come to look for and had prayed for over many years was side-lined by changes beyond our control. Almost like when suddenly the wind shifts and we know that the weather will be stormy, shadowy clouds fill the sky and a terrible blackness seems to settle!

Obedience to that which had been spoken was now set before me and after much prayer and advice from others I took the step of allowing myself to be given into the ground of a further work of grace in my life. It was the hope of my heart that it would bring into the church a fullness of blessing which had been my longing and desire.

This now represents my state of heart at the beginning of the dark journey, it is a time of constant longing and reaching out to heaven. An awareness, where the Holy Spirit draws with deep, deep yearning. Within my heart there is a cry to be taken deeper and deeper in to the power of prayer and deeper into Him.

That same fire which burnt the bush and called Moses forth

for God. The fire that fell upon the altar for Elijah and turned the hearts of Your people back to you. The fire which fell upon the heads of those twelve who first trusted in You for salvation and brought the gospel to the world.

> "Oh God, my God;
>
> In me,
>
> Who is nothing and no-one.
>
> I open all that I am,
>
> To know the all-consuming fire of God;
>
> That in some small way ~
>
> I might become the spark that ignites!"

Here now begins the time of intense difficulty, a time when he comes to take me fully at my word and lifted as it were, the 'lid' off my life. The word that had been spoken to me for the church was now turned towards me personally and it was as though I was to become something of the picture of that which had been spoken.

> "Behold, O My people, I will open your graves and cause you to come up from your graves, and bring you into the land of Israel.
>
> [13] Then you shall know that I am the LORD, when I have opened your graves, O My people, and brought you up from your graves.
>
> Ezekiel 37 v 12 – 14 (NKJV)

There is no easy way for these things to be, no short cuts to God's divine way and His dealings with our lives. One thing is certain my decision to take this step of further opening up my life to the will of God was not greeted with anything but horror, by all those who stood around to watch! In almost an instant I went from being a mature settled Christian, to a complete wreck!! It was as though having given my will up to the hand of God; I stepped into a lift and fell to the bottom of the lift shaft. People looked on in absolute dismay, if this was seeking God's blessing they really didn't want it!

It is so important to stress here, that often it is those who look on and watch, who are instrumental in causing us the most distress when God is working out deep issues within our lives. They are furthermore the people who are least likely to allow themselves to become opened up and vulnerable to the workings of the Holy Spirit, Judgement is freely applied and abundantly given as they stand well back!

As the farmer must plough up his field, the blade sinking deep into the earth turning over soil and reaching down to what lies beneath. So the cross must find entrance and pierce through all that is surface; opening up the life to the 'Divine Blade of God'. In these days I walked over a pathway of stones and like a child turning them over, found all manner of nasty squirmy things hidden beneath!

This was the time when the Lord brought me truly and firstly, into the wilderness place and little did I know what it was to involve and how long it would be for. Those around me continually told me that I was in a 'very bad place' and so I was avoided and side lined in respect to all of the work of the church. My reply to those who stood by with the attitude of dismay was always the same;

<u>"I am not in a bad place, I am in a place of obedience!"</u>
<u>It was my continual statement of faith.</u>

> **"Then Samuel said,**
> **"Does the LORD take pleasure in burnt offerings and sacrifices as much as he does in obedience?**
> **Certainly, obedience is better than sacrifice;**
> **paying attention is better than the fat of rams."**
> **1 Samuel 15 v 22 (ESV)**

When obedience leads us into the wilderness, when the hand of God has lead us into what to others seems the most dreadful mess; the holding of faith and the purposes of God are the only staff that we can use to rest upon and ease the way. No-one, it is certain, who has not walked such a way can ever begin to understand that which, is working out in the life of such a person.

.All had to be set aside as every day seemed to bring a terrible darkness closing in. It was as though I had passed through a portal and entered into another world, where no light falls upon the pathway and nothing can be seen or touched. A deep consuming darkness with no beginning and no end, no place and no time; all becomes the dark journey! It is a great abyss of nothingness, life as it was; has stopped and, it is gone. This is the experience, where laid upon the altar one can only yield and yield to Him. Within my heart there comes a cry to be taken deeper and deeper in to the place of prayer and deeper into You, my Lord and Saviour.

> **"Remember the LORD Your God**
> **"Every commandment which I command you today you must be careful to observe, that you may live and multiply, and go in and possess the land of which the LORD swore to your fathers.**

²And you shall remember that the LORD your God led you all the way these forty years in the wilderness, to humble you and test you, to know what was in your heart, whether you would keep His commandments or not.

³So He humbled you, allowed you to hunger, and fed you with manna which you did not know nor did your fathers know, that He might make you know that man shall not live by bread alone; but man lives by every word that proceeds from the mouth of the LORD. ⁴Your garments did not wear out on you, nor did your foot swell these forty years.

⁵You should know in your heart that as a man chastens his son, so the LORD your God chastens you. ⁶"Therefore you shall keep the commandments of the LORD your God, to walk in His ways and to fear Him.

⁷For the LORD your God is bringing you into a good land, a land of brooks of water, of fountains and springs, that flow out of valleys and hills; ⁸a land of wheat and barley, of vines and fig trees and pomegranates, a land of olive oil and honey; ⁹a land in which you will eat bread without scarcity, in which you will lack nothing; a land whose stones are iron and out of whose hills you can dig copper.

¹⁰When you have eaten and are full, then you shall bless the LORD your God for the good land which He has given you.

Deuteronomy 8 (NKJ)

How it is that when he takes us into a wilderness situation, we must retain and hold on to faith and trust. It is a terrible thing to be in the hand of the living God! Holding on in faith and relying on manna that we do not know; walking in a strange land, each day seeming to be endless and always our vision is only Him,

'He is the Lord.'

Now I began to see myself in a new light, His light! I am all undone by the searching light of God. The light shines through every dark place as He continues to do a deeper work within my life. Many years ago I had given my life to Him, now this was a deeper and relentless searching under His gaze. The Lord drew back the curtain and how dreadful it is to see one's true state. There was nothing much to say as weeping and desperation took over my life. The knife of the Master Surgeon had sliced through my heart and opened up to me everything, hidden beneath the surface.

How many of us go through our Christian life having never really looked at those things pushed down from sight? Gone were the days of carefree blessing, gone was my mature standing in the church, all swept away; all washed away in a tidal wave of distress, as weeping and brokenness took over my life. Each day I woke to more tears as an envelope of darkness, blacker than night its self, had overtaken me.

But through the blackness and the constant distress, I began to see those things that God needed to touch and deal with in order to bring my life again into blessing. It was a process of seeing and placing upon the altar place and allowing the Divine hand to work. He had lifted up the grave stone and now I could only wait while my life was rebuilt again.

It was my testimony that He is and was and will always be the Everlasting, the Almighty God. He is the God who is fire and the God who reigns gloriously. People and things, life and hope, today and tomorrow; pass by like clouds in the sky but there is only Him. The Lord of Glory.

I found that I was able to give Him my trust in this very dark place. I had been like a bird in a cage, banging its wings against the bars in a frenzy to try to escape. There in the darkness, in the prison place I was eventually able to surrender to Him and to His will for me.

Like a sailor cast adrift in stormy seas will cling to a piece of wood, something to keep hold of. I clung to the knowledge that in faith and trust I opened this dark place up to God. In obedience to His word I allowed my life to become a place where others looked on with complete disbelief and horror. Surely He will not allow the wind and waves to destroy me completely?

"When the poor and needy seek water,
and there is none,
and their tongue is parched with thirst,
I the LORD will answer them;
I the God of Israel will not forsake them.
[18] I will open rivers on the bare heights,
and fountains in the midst of the valleys.
I will make the wilderness a pool of water,
and the dry land springs of water.

[19] I will put in the wilderness the cedar,
the acacia, the myrtle, and the olive.
I will set in the desert the cypress,
the plane and the pine together,

> [20] **that they may see and know,**
> **may consider and understand together,**
> **that the hand of the LORD has done this,**
> **the Holy One of Israel has created it."**
>
> **Isaiah 41 v 17-20 (ESV)**

It is a strange thing but as I began to find something of peace and resolution in my walk before God; other storm clouds were gathering. For both my husband and I there began to open up very difficult and dark events. Now in these days we found ourselves increasingly shut out of the workings of the church as political direction changed and we were left at odds with many things. We found ourselves to be there working for a church as full time workers, but were excluded from much of direction and decision making.

It was a difficult time when all that had been our joy and our hopes began to crumble into loss. Still I looked to the Lord for His blessing upon the church but more and more we were no longer a part of what was happening around us. Many things were said that were not true, a web of stories circulated that seemed to have been brought from nothing and nowhere. How the enemy loves to bring chaos and grumbling into the midst of the church spreading, that which is a fabrication of truth and distortion.

How dreadful it is when Christians fall out and that which was beautiful and full of grace becomes marred by derision. It was the cry of our hearts to God "Oh help us for we are all but destroyed and the waters lap over the sides of the boat of our lives!" We were sinking into bitter and stormy waters, there was no-one to stand by us, no hand of compassion. All deserted us, except for a few brave souls who held on to truth against a bitter tidal flow, and with regard to church; we were left alone.

Yet God, is righteous and full of grace, to Him and no other we find ourselves cast for mercy .Days were very hard and we knew not where it would end, yet still in my heart the vision stayed and hope that there would be a move of God continued to be. I had nothing else in my heart, no liberty to pray for anything else; there is only the place of vision and the glory of it. Do I say there is only? For it is a glorious place, filled with the light of heaven, opening out upon people; like oil running over and the air is filled with the sweetness of the fragrance of heaven. My heart continued to hope and believe that resolution would be found.

> **"If it had not been the LORD who was on our side—**
> **let Israel now say—**
> **² if it had not been the LORD who was on our side**
> **when people rose up against us,**
> **³ then they would have swallowed us up alive,**
> **when their anger was kindled against us;**
>
> **⁴ then the flood would have swept us away,**
> **the torrent would have gone over us;**
> **⁵ then over us would have gone**
> **the raging waters.**
>
> **Psalm 124 (ESV)**

Even as the waters flooded our lives with distress and uncertainty, yet the Lord has come again and again to lift and restore our souls. Again and again we found ourselves to be in conflict with those we loved and had come to serve and gradually we came to realise that we were going to have to withdraw from the church and leave behind the blessing of the work that we had been called to do.

The calling of God for service remains a token of His gracious hand. We cannot know for how long that work is to continue and often it is circumstances, which bring an ending to that begun in God. However always it is His work and His time. We must realise that there are occasions when it would seem to us that, something negative ruined a work of grace because of argument and disarray. That is never the case, He continues to be in absolute control, even when it seems to be the opposite!

It was a terrible time of such awful distress and yet always I kept hoping that somehow there would be a breakthrough and all would be resolved. The door to our flat was closed, we were unable now to do those things that had been such a joy and delight to us. In a final stroke of irony, we messaged the church leaders to say that we needed to withdraw; they took it that we were leaving the church. Actually our original intention was to withdraw and rest, we were burnt out and really needed assistance. We had exhausted our resources and were left cast aside and abandoned.

No-one came anymore, it was as though we disappeared and nobody came to look for us. Hard words were said and our position became impossible. That which we had been called to do, to give, to be for the church was swept aside; as the enemy caused a flood of terrible and distressing things to be said and done.

These words from Amy Carmichael seem to summarise the complete unbelief that we had been called to give of ourselves to these people and yet all was lost and washed away so easily. What we began with joy and great expectation; those people which we loved and cared for, suddenly were lost to us and slipped away in the grey mist of a cold winter's day.

"The End"

Will not the end explain?
The crossed endeavour, earnest purpose foiled,
The strange bewilderment of good works spoiled,
The clinging weariness, the inward strain,
Will not the end explain?

Meanwhile He comforteth
Them that are losing patience; 'tis His way
But none can write the words they hear Him say,
For men to read; only they know he saith
Kind words and comforteth.

Not that He doth explain
The mystery that baffleth; but a sense
Husheth the quiet heart, that far, far hence
Lieth a field set thick with golden grain
Wetted in seedling days by many a rain;
The end, it will explain.

(Amy Carmichael ~ Towards Jerusalem)

When we finally let go of our precious things, He is pleased, for those things that we love and treasure can so easily become more than they should be. Church is family, it is home and so much more and now the prospect of this loss was the most terrible of all that I had known.

We were both distressed and confused for all we had ever wanted was to give and be given, working in the calling that was His alone to our hearts. How it is that sometimes that which is beautiful is so hated by the enemy that he will find, always willing hands to pull down and destroy what was given in love.

It is indeed a sacrificial altar where all must be laid down, freely and willingly. There is no clutter upon that altar place, no beautiful candles, no priestly ornate furniture. It is an empty and desolate place where even hope and dreams must be left behind. Is it not so that everything which is laid down and placed here, is consumed by fire from heaven?

Heavenly fire takes up all that we offer and it is received by our Father in heaven. He is pleased when we finally let go of our precious things and we fully yield to Him. Sometimes it happens that we must release our calling and the working of it; time has passed and now we have to let go. That which began with joy and delight ended in heartache, but is it not the way our Lord and Saviour walked before us?

> "**Blessed are those whose strength is in you,
> in whose heart are the highways to Zion.**
> [6] **As they go through the Valley of Baca
> they make it a place of springs;
> the early rain also covers it with pools.**

> ⁷**They go from strength to strength;**
> **each one appears before God in Zion."**

Psalm 84 v 5-7 (ESV)

Is it therefore possible to pass through dense darkness and many perils, making it pools of abundant blessing for those who have put their trust in the Lord Jesus Christ? We have found ourselves hurt in every turn of the road, distressed and cast aside and have now had to take the step of leaving behind the church we came to serve with so much hope and joy!

All but a few people deserted us and turned away and forty years of being in a most wonderful church ended in desolation. Sometimes those things that we love and cherish and are passionate about most of all; have to go, finally put down and walked away from. It is a terrible place of loss, real desperate grief takes over from all that was there before.

But God, thankfully there is always a **'but God!'** and nothing that befalls those who are His can ever destroy us. We are always in His hands and always in His care. Blessed indeed is the man or woman who put their trust in Him. There are times when our way is strewn with distress and difficulty and that is real distress and real difficulty and we are as those in the boat when the winds and the waves would have almost destroyed them. This is not a spiritualised atmospheric place where you remain untouched.

During this time our distress was overwhelming, tears shed, hearts broken. Yet did He who walked the world before us not know the ways of men and refused to commit reliance upon them. Terrible distress is real and tangible, not something somewhere in a spiritual cloud, this is the outworking of those days as we struggled to cope and find anything of hope.

But God, He is in the boat, **He does still calm the waters** of destruction and command the wind to cease. Will we hold our faith? Will we continue to trust? Will we allow Him to take us through the stormy waters? Battle is never a quiet affair and new ground cannot be gained without it.

Into this place of lifeless desert there came as it were, a tiny drop of water, it fell from heaven and found lying in the great expanse of nothingness within my heart, a tiny seed. I do not know how, but in my mind somehow it began to grow and it grew into a beautiful flower. I saw it so clearly the vision of it was so intense. It became for me, a pure white rose and all its petals were open from which there was a wonderful and perfect scent, which seemed to flow from heaven itself.

Now in so much awful distress there came to my heart an understanding, that those who would take this flower; holding it close, were able to enter into the exquisiteness of the flower, its perfume brought peace upon all that was distress. Certainly it was the most beautiful flower and I saw it to be, the flower of forgiveness. Now the Lord moved in my heart to make a move and offer as it were an olive branch to those who had turned away from us.

I contacted each person on the leadership team, to offer this opportunity for reconciliation and forgiveness. However there was not even a reply from anyone, hard hearts and backs turned away! Impressed upon my heart at this time was forgiveness, forgiveness.

Sadly there was no-one who was able to receive the gifted flower and its beautiful heavenly petals lay trampled on the hard cold ground. There was no heart for reconciliation from those who we had loved and prayed with and worked alongside. Instead only a silent stony heart, a face turned away a hand withdrawn.

I have given my forgiveness to those who caused us so much distress and my husband also was also moved to do the same. He even went to meet with the leadership, open hearted for a hand which would facilitate healing. Again it fell upon hard stony ground, he returned home, walking like a dead man, white faced and washed out with the stress of it all. We cannot do more, it is laid upon the altar and only God can move in these things.

We worked for nine years at the church as full time helpers, all completely voluntary, we paid our way in expenses and contributed in every way possible to the work of the church. Sadly we found ourselves in a place where we left alone, without even the shake of a hand or a simple thank you. It is the way of things and we should never be surprised at the ways of men.

In the process of time we now moved out of the flat at church and into our own home that we had rented while working for the church. It was a terrible time of deep and awful anguish. We were even hampered by the timing of these things and not wanting to give notice to the tenants in our house right before Christmas we decided to wait until the New Year. In everything we determined to be honourable before God and could not move from the flat at church, for our own relief.

Now the flat which had brought us so much joy and blessing became like a prison place. We were as exiles living up there above the church. All the normal workings of church continued, people coming and going, we watched them from our windows. Through all the season of Christmas they went through their services and joyful events, while we were abandoned upstairs.

Eventually we moved out of the flat over Easter weekend; what a terrible bleak Easter that was. I will never forget, walking our little dog with tears welling up, as the awful darkness covered everything around us. The cold bleak emptiness was like a drowning torrent, an isolation so intense it pierced everything. Now we had no church and so began a new and desolate pathway even deeper into wilderness places.

Near to our house in the town was an Anglican church, there was a system in that church where the bells played hymn tunes at certain times of day. Terrible it was when we first heard those chimes, the words of the songs like a haunting loss of all that was now gone. We were both desolate and entirely alone.

There are places of wilderness so remote and desolate that life can barely survive. For a committed Christian to have no church, nothing at all, is truly a terrible wilderness place. Sunday became the worst day of the week! No meeting and worshipping with the family of God; almost as though suddenly we were outcasts. In all of that time we never stopped hoping that there would be something of reconciliation. Sadly it was not to be and as everyone else at the church now as it were 'moved on with God' we were completely abandoned and forgotten.

I have often wondered how it is that you can leave people behind, distressed and terribly wounded. Those who you have walked with, prayed and hoped with, surely we are a part of each other our lives inexplicably linked into our Lord Jesus Christ? Yet it is so that there appears to be that ability to turn away claiming to 'move on with God' while we leave brother and sister lying in the gutter of hoplessness.

We were three years in our house after we moved out of the flat at church. Most of that time spent in utter distress, broken beyond it is possible to describe. In that time we longed for and hoped that there would be something of closure and resolution to all that had happened to us. Sadly it was not to be and all opportunities for the healing balm to bring help were rejected and lost.

It is very important to make here the point that despite our awful distress and the lack of care we received from those we had been committed to serving, God is not unjust nor is His hand shortened. There are times when all must be fulfilled, no matter how distressing because the higher purposes of God are forever beyond our understanding.

When we are thrown into the waters of confusion, where torrents of bitter actions and biting winds filled up every part of our lives; rationality is in short supply! We cannot see any forward way ahead and behind us there lies nothing but the ruins of what was our joy.

We found it very hard to maintain a place of vision or even faith, holding on with finger tips is the best explanation. Yet it is that God has prepared a way. We do not see it nor do we have anything to even glimpse upon. He is leading and nothing that has occurred is a surprise to Him.

The will and the direction of His hand reaches far beyond that which we see and experience in our limited understanding. Perhaps there are times when he allows situations and actions which occur, not to reveal the lack in another, but for a further way yet unknown. This is where faith and trust have a new level of meaning and we must be careful not to lay blame or regret at the hands of others, all is to be worked according to heavenly purpose, not ours!

Still today in my heart they remain the family given to me by God, bone of bone and flesh of flesh, He took my husband and I together to be a part of the church and therefore a living part of each life there together. It is a mystery I am unable to explain, somehow they were able to move on and forget about us. Perhaps one day there will come a remembering from God?

BURNOUT

It is at this point expedient to write in a comment regarding this term, 'burnout. This is not added in as a trained professional opinion, rather I include it in retrospect having succumbed to its clutches. As a child I most vividly remember a nursery rhyme, one of the many that were given to children to learn, which bore little sense or reason!

> "Old Mother Hubbord,
> Went to the cupboard,
> To get her poor dog a bone.
> But when she got there,
> The cupboard was bare,
> And so the poor dog had none."

Well it didn't make much sense then either! However the underlying principle is more serious, if the cupboard is bare, there is nothing for anybody. As Christians, especially those who work in any kind of ministry, this I now know, is a very real problem. For some strange reason when we become Christians we think we are 'super human' and when we are involved in a work connected with church then we have moved up a further level and now we are invincible!

The term 'burnout' is obviously a technical or medical term for those who have used up all their resources and have nothing left to give. We become worn out from the constant demands to which the work brings and it is our joy and great desire not to let our people down and more importantly God Himself. Why, oh why do we fall into the trap of thinking that He expects this level of continued effort from us? Is it not the case that he has set down within the scriptures that six days we should work and the seventh day is our rest provision?

Unfortunately ministry brings with it an expectation that we are always available and never tired! We never minded that nor did we see the long term danger that we had tumbled into. It is an inevitable trap which we fall willingly and hopelessly into! One of the first things we did when we moved into the flat at church was to utilise some of our savings and buy a caravan. This would then be a place of retreat where we could rest and be away from everything. We found that mainly when we did go away in the van, we just slept and slept, that should have been a warning signal

As I have previously said we worked in the church for nine years and we just loved being there, nothing was too much trouble, serving and giving was our heart position. We worked alongside another couple who had by the time we moved in already been working there for some time. They had the fortunate disposition to require very little rest and possessed an ability to just continue on working, endlessly!

We however, unfortunately did not have those levels of stamina and fell rather short of the high standard of resources they were able to maintain. Unfortunately the church had become accustomed to working with people who required little rest and wanted little support in that way. So it is that the stage was set for our eventual demise!

For the first seven years we actually worked seven days a week with no official day off at all. If things were quiet we would go out and have time away but there was nothing set for our rest. We were a very busy church with activities in the building on most days and into the evenings. The front doors were usually opened by 7:30am and the building would remain available until 10:30 or later at night according to what might be happening.

It worked out that we shared the opening and closing by having a week on and off alternately. When it was our week on keys, it was necessary to be downstairs opening up at 7:30 and then you would need to wait until everyone had cleared at night before eventually locking up sometimes as late as 11pm. Then the building needed to be secured and checked so that no-one was locked in by accident, it did happen once or twice!

These things begin to take their toll and because you love what you are doing, actually the warning signs are missed and your exhaustion begins to creep in upon your almost empty cupboard! By the seventh year of our time working at church the other couple took a well-earned retirement. Now we were on keys every week, with no space to have any rest, but as I have said we loved what we were doing, so that was fine!

But actually it wasn't. We did now eventually ask for a day off and after much discussion, it was agreed, Monday would be our day off. Except nobody was actually told that we were unavailable on that day and we still had to open and close the building! Oh dear, best described as a 'busman's holiday'! What we really needed and what is necessary for everyone working in any kind of ministry' is someone to watch over you! There needs to be a provision of care which requires adequate rest and provision and for that to be protected.

Love must care and love also must provide for those who are working in full time service. There has to be in built someone, as it were to watch over you! This is essential and the lack of it has probably contributed to many Christian workers becoming worn out. No church group ever gains anything from worn out workers, there must be a very real understanding of this fact. It is also inconceivable that we find ourselves even trying to work and work continually, without a built in resting provision. Even God rested on the seventh day, are we superior in strength to Him?

I came to this analogy of a tea bag! We put a teabag in a cup, pour the water on and then squeeze out of it all the strength it has. Then we throw it into the bin and get another for next time! That is how we felt when we actually withdrew eventually from the work of the church. We were thrown into the bin having exhausted all of our strength and resources.

As I have said we really only wanted to withdraw and have some time out. Someone should have come alongside us and told us to disappear for at least a month, or two and have a complete time of rest. In truth when you are as worn out as we were, you start to become a bit unstable anyway. Some of the issues that went on at that time could well have been because we were too exhausted to process things sensibly and there was no-one who saw that and offered any assistance.

When we did withdraw the leaders had to set up a rota for opening and closing the building. If they had even offered that on our supposed day off, what a difference it would have made. As it was, for the first few weeks after we withdrew, mainly we slept. We just couldn't get up in a morning the full extent of the exhaustion just overwhelmed us.

These things are real pitfalls to consider when working in ministry or being in a position to support those who do. It's very simple we are actually not designed to be invincible, it was never in His plan for us and when we work outside of that which He establishes we will not do well. For us and for those in similar positions you become so absorbed in the responsibility of the work you are called to do, it is a wonderful privilege to serve and be given for the work of the church and the needs of the flock.

However as you read these words, take heed and whatever your place of service or the call that stirs your heart, He has not and will not make you into a super human!

Within the church it is so important for everyone to be aware and sensitive to the needs of each other. It is so necessary for each person to support those who stand next to us and make provision of respect to ensure their facility of time away to rest and recuperate. For both of us the ending of our time of church ministry became a tsunami of distress, much of which was possibly triggered by extreme exhaustion, in short the cupboard was empty and we were beyond having the strength to obtain fresh supplies.

Finding oneself burnt out has long lasting health repercussions which as we are older become far more difficult to navigate. This we have found to our great concern, my husband's health collapsed after the stress of leaving the church and has never recovered. It is so very important for those who work and serve within the church environment to be given adequate protection and tangible care.

As I have previously said there were a few who bravely stood by us and have continued so to do. Not easy when you risk the displeasure of those who look on with disapproval and they certainly were not unhappy with our eventual removal. It was even said to us by some, that they were devastated by all that had happened to us, but they were too afraid to speak or do anything in case they too found themselves cast aside. A very sad state indeed within the church of Jesus Christ where all is supposed to be love and care!

Airbrushed we were out of their lives, all responsibility dispatched and into the bin we went! Fortunately for us, our blessed Lord and Saviour does not throw away his workers nor does He turn His face away in their distress. In all things we must be aware that he is Lord, the actions of those we look to for more, He knows too well. We are all human and will in some measure always fail to be there for each other, it is the way of things and we should not be surprised by it.

THE OIL AND THE WINE

"⁸ And the Lord said to Satan, "Have you considered my servant Job, that there is none like him on the earth, a blameless and upright man, who fears God and turns away from evil?"

⁹ Then Satan answered the Lord and said, "Does Job fear God for no reason?

¹⁰ Have you not put a hedge around him and his house and all that he has, on every side?
You have blessed the work of his hands, and his possessions have increased in the land.

¹¹ But stretch out your hand and touch all that he has, and he will curse you to your face."

¹² And the Lord said to Satan,
"Behold, all that he has is in your hand. Only against him do not stretch out your hand."

Job 1 v 8-12 (ESV))

The Oil & the Wine

Ravaged we were ~
Everything that our lives had been,
Stripped away with ruthless force.
Day after day,
Hour by hour,
No mercy to be found here.

The falling away,
Of that which had been so very beautiful,
The establishing of a work in God.
Now, brought down and destroyed.

Lying bleeding in the gutter,
We were left ~
Crying out in despair.
Robbers came and did their worst.
Tears and distress ~
Make no impact here.

There is no pity ~
A barren expanse of loss,
Has overtaken all,
Breaking down every wall.

Only the cry of anguish,
Echoes across this great ensuing vacuum.
A door closed ~
It will never open again!

"³⁰ Jesus replied, "A man was going down from Jerusalem to Jericho, and he fell among robbers, who stripped him and beat him and departed, leaving him half dead.
³¹ Now by chance a priest was going down that road, and when he saw him he passed by on the other side.
³² So likewise a Levite, when he came to the place and saw him, passed by on the other side.
³³ But a Samaritan, as he journeyed, came to where he was, and when he saw him, he had compassion. 34 He went to him and bound up his wounds, pouring on oil and wine"

Luke 10 v 30-34(ESV)

The Priest and the Levite came to look,

A spectacle we became.

Seeing their approach ~

Hope arose!

The possibility of a kindness?

To no avail ~

Only bitter words,

Hurled without mercy.

How it was that the sight of them,

Brought encouragement and hope.

Possibly relief, even rescue?

We thought ~
Now all will be sorted out and put right again.
But this was a false hope,
Set onto uncertain ground.

Their empty words gripped the desolate air.
Life slipping further away.
Nothing had they to give ~
Except disapproval.

We must be very wrong ~
This just doesn't happen to good Christians!
They had nothing to bring,
Except their importance.
Position is everything.

The grand gestures of yesterday,
All the joys of working together ~
Now fallen away.
Eyes averted ~
A distance set.

Lepers, we have become to them!
We no longer stand side by side,
Working and praying together.

"Then Job answered and said:

² "Oh that my vexation were weighed,
and all my calamity laid in the balances!

³ For then it would be heavier than the sand of the sea;
therefore my words have been rash.

⁴ For the arrows of the Almighty are in me;
my spirit drinks their poison;
the terrors of God are arrayed against me."

Job 6 v 2-4 (ESV)

When the little boat of our lives was crushed,
Battered against the rocks by stormy seas.
Life clinging on in peril,
The darkness of a long weary night.

How they wanted us ~
Just to be gone.
An irritation we were,
To their peaceful life!

Oh, the great horror!
The terrible reality dawns,
Utter complete loss.
Now they are gone,
Disappeared into the night.

They were blown away,
Upon the winds of infirmity.
We placed so much hope onto who they were.
What they were.
Trust had been given ~
The expectation of something ~
So much more.

They passed us by ~
Very spiritually ~
With noble faces set!
Reason has her own account.

In the anguish of this expanding horror,
The garment of our lives,
Mercilessly torn away.
The soul sinks ~
Courage is extinguished.
The inflicted wounds take their toll,

Oh! The endless blessings of mercy!
Is given by 'ONE' who came!
When all was lost and expectation fell away.
Then came, life giving care.

The Oil and The Wine

HE came with the oil and the wine,
He came to restore ~
Pouring blessed grace upon our open wounds.
The oil and the wine was poured ~
To heal and refresh,
Restoration now given.

The' bringer of the oil and the wine,'
The restoration of all that was lost,
He is our nearest neighbour,
Our kinsman ~
Our help, our life.

Never did HE refuse us,
Never would he turn His face away.
He knows the ways of people,
No trust did He put upon them.
They are uncertain hope.

This is the true hope,
Eternally given,
His name is Jesus.
Jesus Christ.

He reigns on high,
This is the Lord of Glory.
When others turned away.
HE CAME!

What we brought,
They did not want.
A more comfortable way was preferred.
No risk here.
No disruption.

The blessing of Jesus Christ,
Must be new every morning.
Life by its own definition ~
Must be growth and even change.
Mana was given, to be fresh each day.

New every morning ~
We must gather his blessings.
New always for His church.
A living church cannot survive on old bread.
New wine, must be given new wine skins.

Change however ~
Is not a welcome visitor.
Always we are happy with the old,
The comfortable.
It is the way of things!

Sometimes, we have perhaps,
Brought too much challenge,
Or possibly ~
Darkness has been given entrance ~
Then so much is lost,
Which was intended for good.
Blessings lost ~
Perhaps for a generation!

"[33] But a Samaritan, as he journeyed, came to where he was, and when he saw him, he had compassion."
Luke 10 v 32 (ESV)

A swathe of awful distress,
Reaching out across time.
It is a scar left, running very deep.
Yet the compassion of our Saviour,
Never is in doubt.

The compassion of our Saviour ~
He knows all ~
Sees all ~

Nothing is hidden.
This is where our trust is set.
Hope eternal will never fail us.

We move forward in that assurance,
A hand that will not fail,
Provision established.

After spending these three years in our house near the church we left the area and moved to another town. We needed to be away from the constant distress which seemed to haunt every corner where we had known such previous joy. Family commitment drew us to another place where help was needed and for us there was need for somewhere perhaps to begin our lives again.

We set out a list of requirements that we needed to look for as house hunting began! These things are never easy! Selling and buying property is one of the most stressful things that people do and we were already very, very stressed!

It is our continual testimony that we were able to buy a house exactly where we needed to be and every box that we had written down was ticked! He does provide and He does always bring His hand of provision over those who are His. Now we had a new page to turn and time for emotional and physical recovery to begin. Our ongoing distress still brought continual difficulty, it really was as though we were outcasts from the family of church.

ITS ALRIGHT TO BE CAST OUT!

These words, spoken to me during this time of great distress; are grace and mercy for that wandering soul for whom the wilderness has become their place of journeying. How we yearn to be out of the terrible situation and want only to find again those things which we once knew and loved and held dear.

Visiting new and different churches was also distressing, it highlighted the way that we didn't seem to quite fit anywhere. We were, it seemed in a strange land with new customs and ideas, new ways to do things. There is new food to eat and new language to learn. How we hate it to be different and want only what we knew to be there again. Even the Children of Israel longed for the 'flesh pots' of Egypt after they were wonderfully removed from its grip. That which we know is always what we really want and where we want to be.

We had assumed that part of moving on was to be a new church to call home, a new family to pray with and work alongside. It is so often the case that we make these assumptions, mainly from our own expectations, rather than an insight into the divine.

The further purposes of that heavenly plan, for a period of time perhaps are removed and hidden away. Always we think and move from the earthly, while the workings of God are, perhaps obviously somewhat beyond our immediate understanding!

"IT'S ALL RIGHT TO BE CAST OUT!"

These were the words that now came to me as we struggled with our new and desolate situation.

It's all right to be cast out!

Moses the servant of God, was cast out,
Cast out from all he knew,
All that had been his life and experience.
He could not have known ~
That in the wisdom of God he would still after many years
Find fulfilment in the call of God upon his life.

In difficult circumstances,
He was forced to adapt and live a new life in another place.
Their ways and their customs were different,
There was nothing to touch upon that was real to him;
Nothing familiar anywhere.

Joseph, a man called from his youth,
To be the implementation of the hand of God,
Was cast out ~
He too had to find a way to live, in a new and strange place.
There was much distress and hardship,
Times of great difficulty.
He was in many ways, an abandoned soul!

Daniel the servant of God,
He too was cast out and carried away.
There was a new land,
A new culture and religious regime,
A new language to learn.
He had not even the freedom to make his own choices,
Everything had to be worked and earned for him to live.

All of these were cast out;
They were cast out,
From the place of knowing ~
The life
The calling
And the certain future that they had expected
They had to learn to live in a strange land.

It's all right to be cast out;
Because in the wisdom and the purposes of God;
He has seen where He needs to send His servants,
So that all righteous might be fulfilled!
There is no waste in God ~
There are no mistakes!

He sends forth and He calls in.
He is The Good Shepherd who knows best in which field His sheep need to be,
In order that all may prosper and that a wider horizon of God might be fulfilled!

A tree flings its seeds wide,
Far away they may be carried by winds and birds and whatever may be a willing vehicle.
Falling into new earth they must then find the means of survival,
Life must always go on!

They cannot mutter and complain,
That this ground on which they fell,
Is not the same as they had known by the mother tree.
Rather they must bury themselves down,
Into the strange earth and wait for rain and sunshine to do their work.

So now ~
There needs to be the recognition,
That we too, can at last be able to bury ourselves down,
Into this strange ground and wait ~
For His hand,
His Spirit~
To do their work upon the seed of our lives!

It's all right to be cast out,
For He alone does the casting,
No hand of man,
No work of darkness.
He alone will work,
To do that which is only and always ~
His the Divine purpose for our lives.

It's all right to be cast out,
For was not He Himself rejected,
Cast out by those that He had come to serve?

We too must find peace and be still,
In order that the perfect will of God,
Might be fully and completely worked through,
Beyond the limits of our human understanding.

He will make a way~
Where there appears to be no way.
He will bring glory and wonderful fulfilment to our lives,
If we give to Him our trust.

It is for us to be abandoned to His will,
His purpose,
Then allow Him ~
To do all that is in His heart to complete.

It is all of Him.

A VOICE IN THE WILDERNESS

"A voice cries:
"In the wilderness prepare the way of the LORD;
make straight in the desert a highway for our God.

[4] Every valley shall be lifted up,
and every mountain and hill be made low;
the uneven ground shall become level,
and the rough places a plain.

[5] And the glory of the LORD shall be revealed,
and all flesh shall see it together,
for the mouth of the LORD has spoken."

The Word of God Stands Forever

[6] A voice says, "Cry!"

Isaiah 40 v 3-6 (ESV)

Our exit from the life to which we had been deeply involved, living in the flat at church took a terrible emotional toll upon our lives. We were cast adrift and alone and as time went on, the broader extent of its full effect impacted more widely upon our every day. During this period; for both of us, there was the entering into desolate wilderness, the void where nothing could be reached or touched anywhere.

We were both in enormous difficulty, but for me still I held to the place of vision. Unmoved by our daily distress I continued to pray for blessing upon the church. Such was the deep and continuing burden of prayer, nothing of our situation changed that, even if I was not to be a part of it. It was my constant, never-ending prayer. I could not understand why I had this urgent and all-consuming passion within my heart; to pray, yet there was no blessing and no interest for it, from what had been our church and those we loved.

In these forsaken days, as we began visiting new churches it became very clear, it was not going to be easy to find a new church. We were looking for a place where we could stay and begin a new life. What we found was that most of the churches we looked at were either completely dead or that hidden beneath the surface of what appeared to be perhaps a modern lively church, was control and a place where there was no freedom to move in the Holy Spirit. It was a shock. We had not looked at what was happening in other churches for many years and now our circumstances brought us up face to face with the 'church' as it is today.

When we were forced to move away from the church where we had known so much blessing, it was a devastating time of brokenness and heartache. It is only now, looking back upon an experience where I know the healing and the fullness of the hand of God that I can begin to find understanding and look again with new eyes at how things are.

There are times in our Christian walk when we pass through troubled waters, perhaps without any awareness of why this or that has occurred. We only know that we are left lying by the roadside battered and bruised and we need someone to come along and pour in the oil and the wine.

"If only!" is the great cry of our hearts. If only this had not happened and if only others had behaved differently. It is a lost cause to which we will never find the answer. The Lord, our Lord Jesus Christ was never in the habit of explaining himself and why would we look for that to change, just for you or just for me?

A good soldier obeys his orders and simply follows instructions. He does not expect the reason for the battle plan to be explained to him. He only follows orders, which is his expectation. The Centurion who came to Jesus asking for his servant to be healed, did not expect that Jesus would need to go to the house with him.

> " But the centurion replied, "Lord, I am not worthy to have you come under my roof! Instead, just say the word and my servant will be healed. [9] For I too am a man under authority, with soldiers under me. I say to this one, 'Go!' and he goes, and to another 'Come!' and he comes, and to my slave 'Do this!' and he does it." [10] When Jesus heard this he was amazed and said to those who followed him, "I tell you the truth, I have not found such faith in anyone in Israel! "
>
> **Matthew 8 v8-10 (ESV)**

As Christians we are in effect soldiers for Christ and in that understanding there will be times when we are suddenly in difficult and unexpected circumstances. The whirlpool of devastation takes its hold and we are carried into places to which we would rather not have found ourselves. How it is that these are the times when all of our resolve is put to the test. The very brave words of commitment and abandonment, oh how they come rushing back to haunt the battered heart. He does not explain, this is a time to trust, we must find that ground where there used to be a simple and quiet faith. He will never, ever abandon those who are HIS!

For my husband and I the battering was intense and faith seemed to be even slipping away. How the fingertips hold on in desperation as the ground falls away and opening up below is a great bottomless pit! There is no dressing up this level of distress nor can you remain intact when the storm winds blow.

All I can say is that HE held onto us and HE kept us when we no longer were able to keep ourselves from falling. Always it is the Lord who does the holding and the keeping, never delude yourself in thinking that you will be strong enough. You will not!

What I now know and see is that the passion that I had for my church previously and the vision for blessing to fall upon it again, has changed. Now that passion is not just for one particular church and group of people, now the passion is for 'THE CHURCH' HIS church.

Those things that He has worked within my life and my heart; the time lost in wilderness distress has given to me this ground, where now I can say with confidence that I have become a voice crying in the wilderness!

Those words that He gives into my heart, HIS words, they are, the outworking of time spent alone and time spent listening. There is no-one to speak them to, no church nor any Christian contact, the words continue to flow as the living waters of His Spirit also continue to flow.

There in my heart is the all-consuming passion for church and for church to be free, so that there might really be the flowing of blessing out to those who are lost. How are the lost ever going to find the life of Christ if the church has lost that place where the absolute reality of meeting with Jesus Christ has been watered down into singing a few catchy songs?

What do we actually expect from our going to church? Have we as Christians lost that place where church was an amazing meeting with the living God? These and many more are the questions that I grapple with as we continue to visit churches in our searching for a spiritual home once more.

When the Holy Spirit moved upon me to bring the words "Its Alright to be Cast out" I had assumed for quite a long time, that finding a new church was the new ground to which the words referred. It seemed necessary to have a new church and in that church to become as it were buried down in order to grow and find new roots once more.

More recently I have however realised that the ground into which Our Lord of Glory was leading me into was in fact. HIMSELF! He has so radically changed my understanding of these things and in working and leading through the desolation of wilderness experience, I find myself changed completely. There is a sense of absolute peace and a walking with Him in deeper and closer relationship.

Furthermore my husband has recently commented, that he was also aware of the deeper and more personal walk with God that he now has. His reading of the scriptures and receiving of understanding from the Holy Spirit bringing new life and purpose constantly.

All of this being achieved while still very much in a wilderness situation. We have no church, no teaching, nor any Christian fellowship or support from anywhere. Hidden away far from view and yet able to thrive where there would normally be nothing to thrive upon. It is the hidden mana of the Holy Spirit provided for those to whom he has brought into reliance upon His hand and His hand alone.

Apart from the very first book which I actually wrote in the time when I was initially brought into the Kingdom of God. (Grace to MY Soul) Most of my writing has come to me during this time. He leads and He speaks and as I have already commented the flowing of the words brings fresh supplies of insight daily!

The structure of the books, even the titles all have come in the moving of His Spirit. They are actually sequential in their outlook and reference, relating the actual wilderness journey as it has occurred. So it has been that the words written during this time reflect the journey and all of its varied challenges.

Sometimes I wake in the night with words flooding through my mind, at other times they come as I sit at the computer typing away. I read a sentence of scripture and suddenly I am flooded with the light of His Holy Spirit upon my way and then the words come to express where I am. His words flow on the wings of His Spirit, while for myself I just write down as they formulate within my mind. This is the fruit of the wilderness experience, where the waiting and listening heart finds the wonders of His grace and mercy to be given.

I have no idea how long this traveling in wilderness terrain will extend. In the beginning, I just wanted it to come to an end so that normality would return. Never-the-less, I ask myself, "What is normality?" Now there is a contentment and a purpose as I walk with Him. The landscape which I thought was barren and unyielding, is now rather a dynamic purposeful relationship in the presence of God.

ADDENDUM TO THE DARK JOURNEY

As you continue reading through these pages, it may have occurred to you to wonder, what actually happened with regard to the 'dark journey'? All the ensuing difficulties which suddenly overtook our lives and nothing further mentioned concerning the outcome of this situation. As it so often the case when the storm winds blow and we are hit by a tsunami of distress, other things pale into the background! Of course He never stops His work upon our lives but we ourselves are perhaps distracted for a period of time.

It is my learned experience, that if we truly and completely give up all of our will to the Lord Jesus Christ, He will never ever fail us. Always and forever our best and fullest interest, He is working to complete. When I entered the time that I have referred to as 'the dark journey', it brought as I have previously recorded a terrible cost and opening up of turmoil to my life.

However, our Lord, was not engaged with these passing moments. His purpose was set on a further horizon, hidden away from my conscious mind and out of sight from my personal awareness. So often in the deep workings of emotional distress, we are unaware of the initial origin and where basically it all began.

Something has been covered over and is now lost to our sight, yet there may be, a certain unease, that perhaps keeps on happening and we have no idea why. Like a hidden thorn buried down, sharp and ruthless it lies, while now and then there will be an occurrence, which becomes a trigger and we are pricked to the core.

Why, we have no idea and gradually we allow its remembrance to drift away again, until a further happening which brings the returning sharp prick to our attention. Poisonous and harsh are its properties, while hidden away out of sight its deathly life lies waiting and as it were asleep, until the next time it will be unexpectedly awakened.

When I entered the dark journey, it was as a result of direct obedience to what I believed to be the word of God spoken to me in prophecy. You see, He knew, what I did not know and saw what I did not see. It is so often the case for us, in our limited scope of vision and even personal awareness.

During this extended time of personal seeking and recollection, I became gradually aware that lurking below the surface of my life there was a hidden fear. Its action crippled the freedom that I had as a born again Christian filled with the Holy Spirit. I had no idea why, knowing that I had always been fully open before God and there was nothing that I had purposely kept back from Him.

We are indeed complex creatures and many I am sure will be able to recognise the situation that began to unfold now in these days for me. For one reason or other our pathway through life inflicts its share of emotional hurt and a tangle of myriad difficulties that we have tried our best to deal with and so often abysmally failed so to do!

I had no idea that a deep hidden fear had been birthed far away from a seed planted in childhood. In fact I had no idea that I had a crippling hidden fear! For all of my adult life it had remained so deeply hidden that anything to do with its memory was now far from my recollection.

In my life as a born again Christian, I began to see that I had a fear of being wrong. I was confident, active and blessed in all aspects of church life and worship. However I would never have been the first to stand up and worship, always I held back a bit watching what others did. Just in case my timing was a bit wrong I often waited and held back. Sometimes I wondered, why would you do that in the freedom of the Holy Spirit?

Our Heavenly Father is so gracious in His dealings with the deep places of our .lives. He always knew and saw a problem hidden away, yet he waited until the time was right. This time being 'right' has nothing to do with the actions of those around us and the seeming chaos that they can bring. Rather it is a waiting on a place where faith has matured and obedience is set, while our lives are as it were laid upon the altar place of abandonment to Him.

In many ways, a bit like an awful experience at the dentist, we can all identify with that one! The tooth is painful, we are perhaps even unwell but facing up to the inevitable removal of the troublesome tooth, well that is another story! We set out with brave intentions and crumble as soon as the dentist approaches with implements in hand!

Another aspect of the deep working of God in my life at this time was the upset and turmoil which then beset our lives. Far even beyond the distress of personal experience, suddenly it was 'open season' and the enemy certainly did not hold back. Perhaps we should keep a mental note that if it is that we are under siege from enemy attack and all the world has turned against us. Then God must be working something wonderful in our lives! I must try to keep a mental note of that fact!

The difficulties which overtook our lives in the last days of our working at the church brought a diversion to the full work of grace which God had prepared and intended for me at that time. So it was that the resulting emotional trauma of our demise of church life hampered the flow of the work of God. It is one of those divine mysteries, perhaps He always had seen that it would be so. I can only know and state, that our Lord did not stop His workings in my life. The 'tooth' had to be extracted the only difference being, the time and place!

In this way, after the trauma of leaving church had begun to settle, I found myself once more needing to find help to both navigate the emotional fall out, from church and negotiate the removal of the troubling 'tooth'! It is so important to accept that help and guidance which others are able and gifted to bring across our pathway. These things are God given, as He brings across our way exactly the right person who has the skills to bring into our pathway all that is required.

It is now to my complete astonishment that I can record and express the gracious work of the Holy Spirit in our lives and the subsequent outworking of His perfect work and blessing. So it was that having cleared the emotional trauma inflicted by the happenings at our exit from church life I became increasingly aware that my Heavenly Father had not yet finished His working in my life.

A light does indeed shine in the darkness and as the scriptures tell us, the darkness is unable to put it out. The probing light of God shines into every dark corner, every hidden place, clearing away the cobwebs of the years. How in every miniscule detail He knows and sees our all, while still recognising the frailty of our lives. In short, He knows **'what makes us tick!'** Yet more. He also knows what is preventing a true rhythm in the **'tick tock'** of our deepest life.

The light now shone, oh, the full and perfect vision, the awful opening reality; we see and we know, perhaps for the first time. This is the true light which flows from God and no action of men, no distraction of circumstances can extinguish its ever piercing gaze.

It was so simple, I just suddenly saw a moment from my childhood illuminated. It floated to the surface of my conscious mind like debris now released from its moorings. How we underestimate the moments long lost and covered away by so many other diversions.

For reasons personal to my growing up I had allowed an idea to take its hold in my mind. It basically said **"If I try very hard not to encourage the displeasure of others, I will be in a much better place and not encourage their subsequent anger."** It had planted a seed deep into my life and unconsciously I had continued to avoid the displeasure of others. Trying to be good, became a lifelong goal, bound for failure!

It was a childhood aspiration long forgotten and without my knowledge remained active for most of my adult life. Now I saw and understood how my Heavenly Father was working to bring into my life a new place of freedom, to which I had not yet acquired. When we see our dark places and they are opened up to the shining light of heaven, not only are they very small and powerless, they are dissolved as **The 'Glorious:Presence' moves across our open heart.**

My time which I described when I entered 'the dark journey' continued for a much longer than I would ever have imagined. Perhaps it was not truly in God's will for that time to be so prolonged, but the circumstances that befell our lives caused it to happen. The process of healing, whether delayed or not is however certain in Him who never leaves unfinished what He has begun.

There came a time one Sunday morning in June 2017, when I stood worshipping in a very restrained and predictable church, with Christians who had very spiritual faces but sadly little joy and certainly where the wells of the Holy Spirit were very clogged up! Oh how it is that when He moves all else is lost from view and we are transposed into another realm!

The Holy Spirit moved across my heart, how else can such things be explained? **Suddenly I was free!** I was free in a way that I had never know before deep, deep within my heart there welled up amazing and unstoppable joy! It bubbled up like a free flowing stream and poured out of my heart like fresh and living waters of life.

There in the midst of a very unemotional congregational, I just seemed to explode with life! I clapped my hands I worshipped Him, I could not stop the flow it poured and poured through my heart and I knew that I was healed and I was free of every dark place and every place of fear. Thank you, Thank you was all that I could say. Amazing grace, amazing love poured out upon those who are His. I also must record that I did not care one bit, what anyone else thought of me as with absolute freedom I worshipped on that Sunday morning!

I remember the scripture, where David, as king of Israel became so carried way with pleasure and worship, dancing with joy over the workings of His God. However his wife, on seeing the actions of abandonment being displayed by her husband, looked on with disapproval. Consequently her displeasure brought repercussions from God, to which she would carry for the rest of her life. The Lord of Glory is delighted with our worship and our .love of Himself. He is also delighted when we actually lose ourselves in our adoration and worship of Him. It is the whole and perfect will of our Father in Heaven that we are truly released and set free to worship and become established in our new 'born again' identity. Nothing is to remain of our previous lives and most certainly no tentacles unseen and running through into the new life that he has for us.

> "⁶ Then the Spirit of the LORD will rush upon you and you will prophesy with them. You will be changed into a different person.
>
> ⁷ "When these signs have taken place, do whatever your hand finds to do, for God will be with you."
>
> **1 Samuel 10 v 6-7 (ESV)**

When we surrender our lives into the hands of our Heavenly Father, there are times when he leads us along pathways which are very hard to understand. Always the truth is that he sees far beyond our restricted vision and His higher purpose is continually looking to take us further and bring more of His life, His love and His power. We have never arrived and are always travelling forward as the' Heavenly Hand', draws us into the deeper realms of God. This is the wonders of heaven imparted, a continuing work of grace upon a yielded soul.

For those looking on at my life, it was disaster and disgrace, the loss of face and inexplicable collapse. He is not concerned with the impression of those who stand and look. Having given up and surrendered our all to Him, now He freely works within the deep hidden places of our lives.

> 'Thus says the Lord God: "Behold, O My people, I will open your graves and cause you to come up from your graves, and bring you into the land of Israel. ¹³ Then you shall know that I am the Lord, when I have opened your graves, O My people, and brought you up from your graves. ¹⁴ I will put My Spirit in you, and you shall live, and I will place you in your own land. Then you shall know that I, the Lord, have spoken it and performed it," says the Lord.'
>
> **Ezekiel 37 New King James Version (NKJV)**

This is truly the testimony of grace, the words that I was given became eventually that which He accomplished within my own life. It is certainly one thing to receive and speak a word given in God but then we must surely be prepared to allow Him to implement that very word in us. So the word of God is received and given and yielded onto, in order that the full working out of heavenly purpose might be realised. He has indeed opened my grave and removed away the stone of impossibility. Now I can testify that he is the Lord and He has brought up my life into His full purpose.

The vision which He implanted within my heart, deep and all-consuming was translated into a profound experience of intercession. Truly that prayer channelled from this time of waiting upon the hand of God, remains. It is held in the heavenly 'bank', where all is upon the golden altar awaiting the further will and purposes of God. He brings His word and translates that into a place of vision, then further it evolves as the yearning and groaning of fervent prayer births and prepares a work of grace.

When all appears to be most lost, as the world views such things, then surely the workings of the Holy Spirit continue onwards. Silently away from sight hearts are prepared, a touch here and a yearning for something more. The work of grace is established upon heavenly time, we should always remember that fact!

WHERE IS THE WATER LEVEL?

In this new release of the Holy Spirit upon my life, I find myself more and more drawn into the workings of church and what our expectations bring to this experience. Where is the church today in the life and fullness of God? How do we relate to unbelievers to enable them also to find faith and the saving grace of God?

The time of prayer and intercession which was an all-consuming part of my life while we served at our church, is now different. The prayer and intercession is in fact banked! Laid upon the altar where all must be released into and onto the workings of God. Nothing about it has changed, the vision has not gone, and rather my relationship with my Heavenly Father has moved forward.

With that in mind it is now, even while still in a wilderness situation, I am earnestly consumed with the whole aspect of our state as church and the great lack with regard to Spirit filled Christianity. We are in a terrible drought where the living waters have long dried up and the freedom of the Holy Spirit is largely unfamiliar.

This scripture has long spoken to me about the flowing of the Holy Spirit and our awareness of where we stand in these matters as church. Can we look in honesty and respond to this question? So it is that we may ask and take stock of all that is the visible life of Jesus Christ to those who come through our doorway as church.

The request rings out to any who have ears to hear.

Where is the water level?

Where are we as His church?

Water Flowing from the Temple

"47 Then he brought me back to the door of the temple, and behold, water was issuing from below the threshold of the temple toward the east (for the temple faced east). The water was flowing down from below the south end of the threshold of the temple, south of the altar.

² Then he brought me out by way of the north gate and led me around on the outside to the outer gate that faces toward the east; and behold, the water was trickling out on the south side.

³ Going on eastward with a measuring line in his hand, the man measured a thousand cubits, and then led me through the water, and it was ankle-deep.

⁴**Again he measured a thousand, and led me through the water, and it was knee-deep.**

Again he measured a thousand, and led me through the water, and it was waist-deep.

⁵**Again he measured a thousand, and it was a river that I could not pass through, for the water had risen. It was deep enough to swim in, a river that could not be passed through.**

⁶**And he said to me, "Son of man, have you seen this?"**

Ezekiel 47 v 1-5 (ESV)

In our churches today:

- Where is the water level? (Ezekiel 47)
- No water to be seen?
- A trickle?
- Ankle deep?
- Knee deep?
- Waist deep?
- Waters to swim in?

We can be delighted in the trickle if we have been a long time in drought. Then the trickle appears wonderful, if we are not careful it would be very easy to delay there. But we must not stop there. The drought was to prepare us ~ to cause us to thirst after more. It is the longing and thirsting that brought forth the trickle; now we must begin to navigate the waters. It is only as the waters begin to rise that now the trickle becomes strong and vibrant, until we ourselves become lifted up and carried by the powerful and growing torrent.

Then it is that the supremacy of the waters moves the impossible.

The power of the waters we can only yield to, and yield to for it will become that place, where all is touched and covered, transformed. We are indeed unable to stand against this flowing tide. Waters to swim in have taken us a long way from the first trickle, it was so important to continue on.

The waters are the type of the Holy Spirit and it must have that free place of movement. That which began as a trickle will become, waters to swim in if we are truly surrendered into the flow. Surely it must be that where the waters of revival begin to flow; someone, somewhere has been thirsty, really thirsty! It is always the case that no revival occurs, without that sure and certain conditions have been met. Somewhere there will be those, who have prayed and yearned and cried out to God, for the windows of heaven to open.

"How long!" The heart cries.

'Come from the four winds and blow', (Ezekiel 37)

Wind of God blow upon this place so dry and worn out. For somewhere at some time a seed will have been planted and it has become an all-consuming passion! It speaks of the eternal grace of God to continue to revive HIS church and to bring in the souls of the lost. It speaks of the eternal promise to open the windows of heaven and pour and pour out abundant blessings of love; where, even if only one soul is looking, listening, hoping.

He will fulfil all righteousness upon His people and extend His church again and again and again. Amen!

To plunge into the waters, to be utterly abandoned. Here is the place where the Holy Spirit flows and is free to be unhindered by the will and designs of human effort; here is the release of the Spirit. Power for healing and restoration, the fullness of God moving among His people. This is the reality, where humanity touches the throne of God and is blessed abundantly, restored to life; full free and overflowing.

Oh the wonder of this eternal grace. It is ever flowing, a mighty river that cannot be stopped when once the flow has been released.

This is where we must be in the church now ~ waiting ~ watching ~ listening ~ looking!

Having ones senses tuned in, to hear any hint of the breeze beginning to blow ~ to feel perhaps the commencement of the stirring of heaven! While deep within the heart there remains the vision that will not stop, or go, or relent its drawing upon us. It is the eternal workings of grace; in order that HIS church, will be revived. These all-consuming embers wait for the breath of God; will they blow upon our feeble flame? They are waiting for the day of His power.

Are we prepared to take the risk of giving up our control? To begin to live within the church in a place of Spirit filled unexpectability? To yield up and let go, so that the Holy Spirit then is free to manifest an ordered place of wholeness brought by His hand alone. It is the ground where we learn that truly, when God is at work, we must cease.

- When men are at work He will cease.
- When God is at work, then comes the increase.
- **"Son of man, have you seen this?"**v6
- What do we really see?
- What are we really looking for in our churches?
- Week after week after week!!!

NO COMPROMISE

There are some places of truth, beyond which we cannot turn our responsibility away and for that reason it is a place of 'no compromise' from which we must make a stand and make our voice heard. These words speak of His exceeding greatness and power, the riches of His glory and so much more; it is all for the church, His church, His body which is the outworking of all that He is for us all.

"¹⁵ For this reason, because I have heard of your faith in the Lord Jesus and your love toward all the saints,

¹⁶ I do not cease to give thanks for you, remembering you in my prayers,

¹⁷ that the God of our Lord Jesus Christ, the Father of glory, may give you the Spirit of wisdom and of revelation in the knowledge of him,

¹⁸ having the eyes of your hearts enlightened, that you may know what is the hope to which he has called you, what are the riches of his glorious inheritance in the saints,

¹⁹ and what is the immeasurable greatness of his power toward us who believe, according to the working of his great might

²⁰ that he worked in Christ when he raised him from the dead and seated him at his right hand in the heavenly places,

²¹ far above all rule and authority and power and dominion, and above every name that is named, not only in this age but also in the one to come.

²² And he put all things under his feet and gave him as head over all things to the church,

²³ which is his body, the fullness of him who fills all in all."

Ephesians 1 v 17 – 23. (ESV)

If Jesus Christ is truly this fullness, this wonderful filling of all in all; then that truth must apply to all aspects of our life experience as His church. Can that truth be relinquished to the interpretation of a single person, who will make judgement and we accept decisions and practices on that basis? It appears to be a common situation in many churches now; that when the Spirit moves in the heart of a member to minister in the gifting they have received of God, one must 'ask' permission to minister that gift. Then someone in the meeting or service, appointed by the church, will at that moment decide if what someone is about to say, has the correct tone / subject matter / or can be heard at all!

Where oh where is the free abundant moving of the Holy Spirit in all of His grace and power among us? If we are indeed all filled with this fullness, which fills all in all; why then is there so much fear of freedom and the heavy hand of control resting upon believers?

There is a cry that order will be lost and chaos prevail! But He is not a God who brings the spirit of confusion. If we can but trust in Him, He will indeed bring into our gatherings order and blessings beyond our very restricted vision. There is also a cry that 'the vulnerable' will be compromised! But does He not know every heart and what we need to hear Him speaking, even when we are vulnerable?

I remember very clearly in the early days of my faith when, yes I was very vulnerable; but never was I disappointed as I listened for the moving of the Holy Spirit. How clearly I now recall being perhaps in a delicate place, yet hearing someone move in the gifts of the Spirit immediately prompted my heart to listen. "What did God wish to say," I would think, "Has He got something to speak into my situation?" Oh yes, so many times there came words flowing which lifted the troubled heart, encouraged one to get up and carry on. Without the freedom of that ministry I very much doubt I would be where I am today.

If freedom is given for the members of the church to follow the leading of the Spirit, will we not leave ourselves open to all that is 'odd' and 'false' to be spoken. Thus again causing upset to the vulnerable among us. He gives to us who are His, certain principles of spiritual warfare; which we are told, we must **'put on'**!

We must put on these vestments if we intend to function in confidence and maturity in the church. They are given to each believer as protection against the intrusion of the enemy. These are not cloaks and gowns, such as we see in the established church. Very fine they may be, however this now is the 'putting on' of spiritual attributes and the gaining of them must come through the receiving of the Holy Spirit in power for each believer.

In the process of such we learn and begin to develop the ability to discern the workings of the Holy Spirit. This discernment being part of the gifting of the Spirit upon the church. However, as with many things we need to begin to learn 'how to', if we are to grow as Christians. There is a need to begin to learn how to test what is right or wrong. Also to begin to assess what is given for ourselves to appropriate and what is perhaps for another.

If everything we ever hear has been sanctioned and scrutinised by another. How is the believer ever to grow in these things? As with all we ever do there comes a time when we must stand up and begin to walk for ourselves, begin to process what we hear. Every believer needs to make the transition from drinking milk to eating real food. Food that now must be chewed. It is a principal of growth. Otherwise we shall for ever have churches full of Christians who rely entirely on others, to keep them safe and decide what is good and appropriate for them to eat.

When the Spirit of God is moving among His people, must we refer to a man, to ask permission? Do we move in obedience to the Spirit within us or do we go and ask permission first so that we do not cause offence? It is a difficult question, however the outworking of it brings a stifled hand upon the heart and restricted flow in these matters. When the Holy Spirit is able to move freely among the hearts of His people; then the fullness of Him who fills all in all is released to flow, it is as a river flowing, a vast flowing tide of mercy and grace. It brings about a release of power when all are still before the throne and all wait upon His hand.

If people have never had to opportunity to sit before the Lord in freedom and acceptance together as the church, then there is only a partial flow, the waters are held back and the fast flowing deep places of God remain largely unknown. It is a certain fact that what we have never had or known, we will not miss and so therefore only ever be satisfied with what is placed before us. The full release of the Spirit within the church is as a boundless river flowing and when the individual believer is moving in that full flowing water it rises up as a great wave within the heart and we are carried by that wave if we choose so to be!

Regardless of all that went wrong in our time working and serving in our church, there is forever imprinted this principle of freedom to move and experience the fullness of the Holy Spirit. Unfortunately, as with many churches gradually over time we lose the vibrancy of the fullness of that flowing river of God.

We become as it were, silted up, clogged and needing the channels to be cleared! It is sadly part of our humanity, we experience a wonderful move of God and are delighted to be a part of that life. However slowly and mainly unconsciously we cannot keep our hands off the gifting we have been given and so it is that slowly it drifts away from us.

We maintain the pattern which was a living breath of God, yet the more we take that pattern and evolve it into a format, it dissipates quietly away. He must have absolute control, when we take that control despite it retaining many aspects of the life of God, it lacks HIM!

RIDING THE WAVE/ EDDIES & CURRENTS

I have had many conversations with church people in regard to this aspect of being free to minister in the Holy Spirit. The difficulty is always trying to explain the workings of these matters to someone who only knows that control must at all costs be maintained. So it was after yet another conversation about this issue, which ended dismally; there came to me what I can only describe as an image in the Spirit.

In reality, there is a great lack of real Spirit life when we come together as 'church'. There is lots of singing very lively and modern, but is that it? Is that the full and deep moving of the Holy Spirit? Mostly, what constitutes church is planned, scripted, and written down to be read out! Oh such terrible deadness prevails over it all. Much singing and talking and following 'the plan'. No life, no space for the Spirit to move within the meeting of believers.

But most of all no experience of that wonderful presence, who causes the heart to jump as He delights to move and bless His own. In our preoccupation with keeping order and following the plan, we have frozen Him out of our gatherings and our meetings.

Where I did not have the words to express fully this matter, into my heart suddenly came a picture which still today expresses the issue. I saw the impression of a great wave rising up, it came to me, bringing a means of providing a physical representation to that which is invisible. Again and again I am aware of the lack of real freedom to move and minister in the gifts of the Holy Spirit, as the Spirit gives utterance, within the church.

The picture of the great wave came to me as a means of explanation to the workings of these things. An explanation that I myself did not seem to have the words or means to provide. Firstly I saw a man on the beach with his surf board. The waves rolled and crashed randomly across the beach. He waited and watched, he was looking for a wave that he would be able to catch and ride.

He watches, he waits, until suddenly he sees the wave and somehow he knows that this is the one. Eagerly he rushes out with his board to catch the wave. The wave rises higher and higher and at just the right moment he steps out and catches the wave.

This then is the moment, he balances on his board, stands up and allows the power of the wave to move him forward. There now this fragile element not only supports his weight but wonderfully carries him forward as he is abandoned to wherever it will take him.

My question now is, what would happen to the man if he was required to ask permission from 'the beach manager', before he caught the wave? The glorious experience would have been lost. He would never have ridden the wave nor is he likely to ever know that experience for himself!

He may learn to watch the waves, to admire them but he will be unlikely to know the actual experience of riding the wave; because waves do not wait while we rush to ask permission from 'the beach manager'! Waves are like living entities, they appear and move and exert great power, but they are never going to wait for us! We have to catch the moment or else it is gone for ever, the life of it, the power of it has slipped away.

So it is with the Holy Spirit as we meet together as church. If we are to fully embrace the gifts of the Holy Spirit, given to us at Pentecost, we must be like the man who wanted to ride the wave. We wait upon Him, we still our hearts; but when, oh when there is that gracious moving of His Spirit upon us we must be ready to ride the wave!

It takes great courage to step out, to as it were stand up on the board, when He comes to touch our heart ~ we know ~ this wave is for us! Sometimes there will only be a word or two, a tongue may begin to form and somewhere deep down our heart races. The Holy Spirit moves within our hearts and we know without any doubt that He has brought into our heart something of Himself.

We are touched by the Holy Spirit and like the man with his surf board, we have to stand up and begin to ride the wave .At that moment the power of the Spirit rises up within us and we are most wonderfully carried by the energy of its flow. It is an amazing journey to, we know not where! But we must have both the courage to do and the freedom to make that journey.

If our situation demands that we have to ask permission to move, to respond to the promptings of the Spirit, then that living journey; that knowing of the workings of these gifts given to the church, will be stifled. We try to re-create afterwards something that was alive and vibrant and in doing so we lose that living freshness it was designed to have.

It becomes past tense in its deliverance! The Holy Spirit is never such! Our deliverance of a word from the Lord has lost the sparkle of that living moment' when it was birthed in a believing heart and much of the power and the resonance becomes now dulled.

I have seen that, as we come together as the church, it is like a picture of flowing waters. In a great body of water there is the moving of eddies and currents. They move almost unseen within the depths of the water; on the surface we may see only a ripple or flicker within the flow.

However deep down under the water these eddies and currents exert great power. This is the place where the power of the body of water moves most strongly. The swirling movements within the water stir up from the deeps particles and sediments. In this swirling mass they rise and become a food source to the living creatures that make their home in the water.

Oh the picture of this heavenly wonder! For us as we meet together as the church where the Holy Spirit moves freely and powerfully among us bringing a word in season to every waiting heart. Heavenly food from those deep places where His Spirit brings to us the life of God. The church, those who are His, as we come together we become one in the body of Christ and it is in that place where the Holy Spirit is able to move like the swirling currents of the water bringing to one and another that which is the life giving touch from Him to us.

Now like with the waters of the deep, His Spirit moves and flows and breathes within us. It is the living, moving, presence of God, for us ~ the church.

Do we know that to be so as we meet week by week?

Like within the deep waters there flows that' Beautiful Holy Presence'. It flows between us and through us as we open our hearts. Most wonderfully, as with in the water there are eddies and currents that move and touch and stimulate our hearts. When we are touched by this heavenly flow it brings, inspired vision and causes us to know and hear heavenly conversation.

If we are open and abandoned into the power of the flow our hearts will be carried on a heavenly current and the swirling eddies of His Beautiful Presence', cause thought and words and all that is the heart of God for us; to become recognised. The heavenly food is made accessible to all who are listening, we partake of His banquet laid out across our way.

Where the gifts of the Spirit are allowed to function, in trust and abandonment to Him; without restriction by men and systems. Then all are blessed, all may be fed, every heavenly crumb is precious, never to be discarded. In this way where believers have the courage and freedom to be abandoned to the ministry of Jesus Christ. He will not fail to bring to us the deep, deep places of heavenly blessing.

It is not a meeting or a service with great disorder, but rather a place of boundless abandonment where freed hearts may feed and grow into maturity .The Holy Spirit moves among His church touching hearts as they wait upon Him by the inspiration of His living presence moving in the deep eddies and currents of His will.

One may have a message of prophecy, another a tongue and yet another its interpretation, all are for the building up of the church and its members. In this place of freedom they are spoken in life giving freedom, so that we may all grow up in these heavenly things and that He may be glorified in the church of Jesus Christ.

"It is vital that the living stones quarried in times of revival shall not be left lying about, but shall be built into the house of God and share the corporate life of the church. Therefore the form and condition of that local body are of great importance.

It is surely right that a soul converted in revival when the Spirit was in complete sway, should be brought into a fellowship where, in simplicity of apostolic church order, the Spirit continues to control, and where there is scope and liberty for each member to exercise his or her spiritual gifts to the blessing of all. How often the flames of revival have been extinguished by the very structure in which it broke out.

After the first inrush of the Spirit, the doors and windows were shut by the iron hand of ecclesiasticism, formalism, and tradition; the flame was suffocated; the Spirit quenched."

"In The Day of Thy Power"

(Distinctive Features) Arthur Wallis.

IN THE DAY OF HIS POWER!

I do not know how or when or where the vision that has been imprinted upon my heart, for a new move of God in His church, will be released. Now in these days more and more I realise that eternal heavenly time is way beyond our understanding. We really do see through a glass dimly and our assumptions concerning the outworking of the purposes of God, often need to be re-visited as He opens up the road before us. Through the workings of His hand, in the experiences of life, He extends our ability to see, hear and know if we are watching and waiting and listening to the heavenly heart beat!

The dreams of Joseph.

"5 Now Joseph had a dream, and when he told it to his brothers they hated him even more.

6 He said to them, "Hear this dream that I have dreamed: 7 Behold, we were binding sheaves in the field, and behold, my sheaf arose and stood upright. And behold, your sheaves gathered around it and bowed down to my sheaf."

8 His brothers said to him, "Are you indeed to reign over us? Or are you indeed to rule over us?" So they hated him even more for his dreams and for his words.

9 Then he dreamed another dream and told it to his brothers and said, "Behold, I have dreamed another dream. Behold, the sun, the moon, and eleven stars were bowing down to me."

10 But when he told it to his father and to his brothers, his father rebuked him and said to him, "What is this dream that you have dreamed? Shall I and your mother and your brothers indeed come to bow ourselves to the ground before you?"

11 And his brothers were jealous of him, but his father kept the saying in mind."

Genesis 37 v 5-11 (ESV)

"8 And Joseph recognized his brothers, but they did not recognize him.

9 And Joseph remembered the dreams that he had dreamed of them"

Genesis 42 v8 (ESV)

Is it not the case in the working out of heavenly matters; the time between the first glimpse of vision and the fulfilment of that vision is a journey of faith? This is, where God works through His way in the life and the experience of those who are His? Perhaps a lifetime of experience and difficulty, perhaps a sense where it has all been long forgotten. Yet, somewhere and at the absolutely right time there will be that touch of heaven and we will again remember the vision and know faith wonderfully rise.

Joseph was a young, brash youth who had prophetic visions through his dreams. Though the vision was real, the time was not and many years needed to be worked through with much hardship and distress; before all was accomplished. This was the making of a strong man of God, who eventually stood in an attitude of dignity and compassion. From the place of vision there is a long and distant way to be travelled, until it would seem to us that the vision is lost and long forgotten.

It is the pattern of the outworking of the hand of our God; He brings the vision, the word, and the passion for that which is in His heart to do. Then it must be seasoned by the workings of time and eternity. Does He not have all of time for ever? Perhaps we will not even see in our limited life time the outworking of those things to which we were given a heavenly glimpse, but they remain held and fixed waiting for as it were the moving of the waters!

Of one thing we may always be certain, it is in the heart of God to bring upon His church the fullness of His divine hand of blessing. The abundant flowing of heavenly grace was poured out for all of His own at Calvary and that flow is ever ready and always waiting for hearts that can find again the place of seeking and searching for more!

Are we hungry?

Will we leave all that we are and all that we have to again follow Him? Those fishermen long ago took such a step of faith, became for all of us an example, a picture of what can be and how the Holy Spirit is able to transform a life when all the restrictions are removed.

He waits for the heart that will abandon all else and allow the workings of God to fulfil all righteousness!

He is the fullness which brings to His church life and causes the stones that are lying lost and burnt to be picked up and used again. Are we ready for a new move of God? Will we perhaps after many dry years find again that place like the deer who follows the scent of water, the living water flowing for all fresh and free?

Will we search and seek after Him?

For loves sake.

Does your heart hunger and thirst,

For righteousness?

To touch upon the throne

And be taken up with Him

Oh, that we are again ~

Able to hear the heartbeat of heaven!

Moses was 'a perfect child!' his mother looked upon him and instinctively made plans to keep him safe. For that reason he was hidden away for three months while she watched over him daily. While he was hidden he was safe and her child was nourished by her devotional love and care.

When we hold within our hearts a place of vision, it is safe while we hold it close. That which God has birthed within us we nurture as we hold all things in His presence. But as with all everything, there comes the time when our 'perfect child' must be cast upon the waters and released from our touch!

For Moses his mother made a basket and putting all her hopes onto God she pushed him out from her reach. The hopes and yearnings of our hearts eventually have to be released into a place where other forces take control and we have let go and wait for the will of God to be accomplished.

Sometimes even when we have in obedience cast our hope upon the waters, we are given them back to grow and mature until the next time that we will again have to let them go. Moses was set to grow up in privilege and learning, yet still there is the place where his calling and destiny outweigh all else and again, like Joseph he moves from a place of immaturity to function in those things that he is not yet equipped to do.

Moses Flees to Midian

[11] One day, when Moses had grown up, he went out to his people and looked on their burdens, and he saw an Egyptian beating a Hebrew, one of his people.

[12] He looked this way and that, and seeing no one, he struck down the Egyptian and hid him in the sand.

[13] When he went out the next day, behold, two Hebrews were struggling together. And he said to the man in the wrong, "Why do you strike your companion?"

[14] He answered, "Who made you a prince and a judge over us? Do you mean to kill me as you killed the Egyptian?"

> **Then Moses was afraid, and thought, "Surely the thing is known." ¹⁵ When Pharaoh heard of it, he sought to kill Moses. But Moses fled from Pharaoh and stayed in the land of Midian. And he sat down by a well.**
>
> **Exodus 2 v 11-15 (ESV)**

Desperate situations always bring about emotional response and God does not move in the emotional. His calling upon a life for deliverance will only be worked in power and authority and a determination to stay and stand in unyielding confidence before His throne.

Moses has yet to loose himself and find God. He has yet to turn away from the response of the desperate and come to the place of forgetfulness; where all has been covered in dust and sand and the boldness of youth has long relinquished its drive. The cry for deliverance, within the people of God is strong and it is that growing intensity of the groaning of the people of God that brings an awakening in heaven and we are told that God remembers!

Is there today a cry, a groaning from the people of God? Is there a voice that will rise up to heaven and awaken the heart of our God so that great wonders and power might be released to His church?

Moses is looking after sheep when God opens heaven, his situation far removed from the needs of his people. His life has moved on and by our standards he is elderly, past what might be thought of as being eligible for a great work to do. How it is that so often we have to travel far away and lose all that was vision, all that we were looking to happen so wonderfully, those things that we glimpsed upon in younger days have now become lost to us; we have through life's circumstances let them go.

A work of God, must and can only be, a work of God! It is never a work of a man or a woman, having no signature upon it other than the Lord himself. Now at this time Moses responds by saying that he cannot do what God asks of him because he is not able and cannot even speak the words that will be needed.

So it is that where vision or calling or anything of heaven is given to men and women, first there must be the time of preparation, the loss of self and the loss even of the vision. All must be pushed out upon the waters and allowed to be carried away by life's currents where storm and sand and wind will work and take all things out of the hand of a man or a woman and laid upon the altar place.

The place of vision must become that which is laid down and even tied upon the altar place. Perhaps our work in all of the matter, was to hold the vision and to pray, to be that voice in the wilderness crying out to heaven. Now the voice is lost and there is nothing more to say, life has moved on.

But there upon the altar place,

Most wonderfully.

Is every prayer,

Every cry and hope that we carried,

For all of those years.

The tears of the years,

Wonderfully filling the trench around the altar,

The searching and longing ~

Layer upon layer,

All there, nothing has been lost!

It is an amazing truth that the workings of God are beyond the understanding of our humanity, how we would have rushed it all and lost the wonder of it. Now all is of God and all is in God and there is a time set in eternity when the fire of heaven will fall, we wait and we watch, but our part has been played. The fulfilment and the outpouring, that wonderful moment when the windows of heaven will eventually be opened has been set and glory will once again fall upon His church.

Then there will be those who will ask, "Where did this come from and how has it been worked?" Only a few will know the answer, those who have put their hand to the plough along the way. They will know and they will be able to answer; "It is the will of God to move upon His people now at this time, this is the day of His power!"

"In the six hundredth year of Noah's life, in the second month, on the seventeenth day of the month, on that day all the fountains of the great deep burst forth, and the windows of the heavens were opened."

Genesis 7 v11 (ESV)

CONCLUDING THOUGHTS

It is very important to write certain words in reflexion of all that occurred to us during the years which this writing represents. It was indeed a journey along a road, opened in following the call of God and the subsequent difficulties experienced during the following of that road. There is no guarantee that because we follow our Lord Jesus Christ and His calling upon our lives, all will be as a 'bed of roses!' The actions of people who we thought were working alongside us and shared a like vision, on occasion brings disappointment and even disagreement.

In the context of church and the hope of faith, there are times when Christians fall out and we are suddenly cast upon a stormy shore. Always there is the hope of reconciliation, though the hardness of our hearts can make this very hard to facilitate. Never-the-less, it is important to also remember that the heart of Pharaoh was made stubborn by God in order for Him to work through a greater good and a more wonderful transformation for His people.

So in that way, there are times when it would seem that God looked the other way and allowed us to be cast upon the waves of the storm. The brothers of Joseph sold him into slavery, yet this was the outworking of the heavenly purpose for years not yet fulfilled.

Those difficulties which we encountered through the action of persons we loved and were devoted to serve, they are ripples in the great sea of heavenly will and the further provision, yet to become revealed. We were abandoned in great distress but we found a deeper and richer fullness than we had known previously. He never abandons those who are His, we however need to learn new and deeper ways to walk where the reliance upon men slips away.

This is truly His perfect will, looking onto Him and Him alone, we are never disappointed nor will we ever be let down. We have no regret in our following after the Lord and responding to His call upon our lives, regardless of all that ensued in the aftermath of those years.

The Lord knows those who are His and given into His perfect will. It is a privilege to have served and to have known the calling into that service. We are forever upon the altar place for His will to be fulfilled. He is the Lord and glorious are His ways beyond our understanding.

We wait upon His perfect will and trust in the outworking of the purposes of God in order that all of righteousness might truly be fulfilled. Now in these days where church continues to appear lost in a whirl of social modernity, so much more we need to find again the breath of heaven. Can we, will we as the church of Jesus Christ rise up once more renewed and refreshed to speak life and faith to a new generation?

THE STRONGHOLDS OF THE WILDERNESS

"And David remained in the strongholds in the wilderness, in the hill country of the wilderness of Ziph. And Saul sought him every day, but God did not give him into his hand".

.1 Samuel 23 v 14-15 (ESV)

In the land of great emptiness,
Where men fear to tread.
In barren sands of endless nothing ~
Where harsh winds blow.

A man, a woman may walk,
Not by choice ~
Nor with any thought of comfort.
Never in the search of beauty.
This is a landscape lost and relentless,
No loveliness lingers here.

Only a few, walk this way.
Not many ~
Would hold aspiration, for this pathway.
The solitary soul ~
Battered by vicious squalls of circumstance ~
Hedged in ~
With all other options closed.

This is not an elected passage.
The situations of life,
Now prevent every other way.

HE, designed it so to be!

A person here ~
A door slammed there ~
A desperate situation!

No hand of compassion.
Faces turned away ~
Oh, the endless pain!

BUT GOD!
There is always ~
But God!
Thankfully!

He has chosen for me,
Perhaps for you also,
This special journey.
All of the engulfing distresses,
Every hard place ~
It is ~
Driven by heavenly purpose.

Each way closed ~
It was a door opening.
To HIM who is Spirit and Life.
Entrance we now find,
Into the deep places,
Of God.

Softly, in the still and clinging air ~
We catch the scent of something,
It drifts through,
Upon waves of heavenly sweetness,
Filling our silent universe,

It is His way,
It is His will.
The Heavenly Hand ~
Beckons us ever onwards.

No man has caused this to be ~
No unkind words or actions.
This is God given,
A way of divine preparation.

Blinded we were and distressed.
"I am alone!"
Was the hearts cry.
Alone indeed, was our perception ~
A terrible desperate isolation,
But never was it so.

We were turned by invisible forces,
In to the wilderness way.
To walk an empty void.
So that we may discover ~

That to which many, never see or know,
Nor have perhaps touched upon.

The journey began alone.
A heart closed in.
No-one to reach or touch upon.
Oh, the anguish of separation,
From all that used to be.

Grief has bitter tears,
While the agony of loss,
Tares away at a soft heart.

Yet our tears ~
They fall upon the sterile sand,
Quickly lost and dispersed from view,

In this dry unforgiving land.
They seem to be as nothing ~
Absorbed by an unseen hand!

It was never His intention,
For us to remain overwhelmed by our distress.
The desert has a way,
Of continually removing and draining dry,
Every last droplet of pain ~
That slipped from a broken heart.

DO NOT LINGER HERE!
DO NOT ALLOW LOSS TO BECOME THE MASTER.
NEITHER GIVE RESENTMENT ANY SPACE!
LOOKING BACK HAS NEVER BROUGHT GOOD RESULTS.
That we know very well!

"At dawn the angels hurried Lot along, saying, "Get going! Take your wife and your two daughters who are here, or else you will be destroyed when the city is judged!"
[16] When Lot hesitated, the men grabbed his hand and the hands of his wife and two daughters because the Lord had compassion on them.
They led them away and placed them outside the city.
[17] When they had brought them outside, they said,
"Run for your lives! Don't look behind you or stop anywhere in the valley!
Escape to the mountains or you will be destroyed!"
Genesis 19 v 15 – 17 (ESV)

[26] But Lot's wife looked back longingly and was turned into a pillar of salt.
Genesis 19 v 26 (ESV)

We must make the challenging resolution,
Longing, is the great temptation?
The cucumbers of Egypt, beckon to us!

We make the choice,
To look up!
Now quietly, gradually, it all begins to fall away.

We let go,
Of the garment of distress ~
Oh there is a great release.
His hand was there all the time!

Eventually we will discover ~
There is a great hidden wonder,
Here within the void.

Loss is turned into increase.
Grief becomes mellowed.

In the solitary place,
We recognise ~
That we are actually not alone!
Nor abandoned,
As we had previously thought.

There are strongholds in the wilderness!
Safe and protected we now are.
Do you know that?
Have you discovered it for yourself?

We must remain in the stronghold.
It is God given.
A rock of safety,
Our defence from enemy attack.

Here upon this **'ROCK'**~
Eternity is being worked.
The purposes of God fulfilled

Only His provision counts here,
From God's hand ~
To my mouth ~
To my heart.
Now I know, I see,
Beauty has filled the desolation.

All that was ever loss,
Those things that were deemed to be important,
The invariable issues of life,
Even the delights of belonging ~
Being an active part,
How I find myself to be amazed.

The stronghold of the wilderness,
This very safe place,
Where the hand of the enemy is prevented.
It is a heavenly way.

Golden and beautiful is the sand now!
My heart ~ changed!

In the wilderness stronghold,
Heavenly arms enclose.
There is a meeting with HIM.

Now the bitter winds cease,
Silence is indeed, golden!
We are lifted up ~
Into a higher place,
A great vista opening up.

We will remain in this stronghold,
Until heavenly purpose has been fulfilled.
The rock of escape is our grounding now.

Upon this 'ROCK' we will forever stand.
Never again will we fear the solitary way,
Nor will the bitter winds tare at our heart.

Other issues will cause offence.
It is life's way.
There will be hardship and even grief,
We cannot escape the inevitable.

Yet as we now continue forwards,
We will discover ~
In knowing the stronghold ~
In finding, the 'rock of escape'
We found eternal strength.

Oh, I want you to know!
That even as the relentless howling winds,
Tore every precious thing away,
Mercilessly stripped, beauty and hope.
Refused to hear the cry of despair.

There was always 'One,'
Who looked down and knew!
One to whom the hearts of men held no surprise.
From HIM ~
Came only an open hand of mercy,
A constant flowing stream of grace

Oh, I want to say to you,
My fellow traveller.
That of this you may be certain,

No insensitive hand,
No voice of threat,
Nor any situation,
Bringing down all of cherished hopes ~
Can ever separate you ~
From your precious Lord.

This is the stronghold of faith ~

The knowing of HIM.
To be in His Presence!

When all the noise of the battle has ceased.
Every fallen stone lying scattered around,
Here in a broken world of pain ~

HE HAS COME!

Lord Jesus YOU have come.
Bless the Lord Oh, my soul,
Lord Jesus You have come.

Pouring out the oil and the wine,
Bless the Lord, Oh my soul.
You have healed a broken heart,
And now ~
My face does indeed shine!

Now in the wilderness way,
A heart finds peace.
A beautiful transforming joy.
It is the gift of God.

Fellow traveller ~
In the desolate empty void,
In a land of bitter winds ~
We are overtaken by beauty
Forever established,
By the hand of our Lords Jesus Christ.

"⁷ But whatever gain I had,
I counted as loss for the sake of Christ.
⁸ Indeed, I count everything as loss because of the surpassing worth of knowing Christ Jesus my Lord. For his sake I have suffered the loss of all things and count them as rubbish, in order that I may gain Christ
⁹ and be found in him, not having a righteousness of my own that comes from the law, but that which comes through faith in Christ, the righteousness from God that depends on faith—
¹⁰ that I may know him and the power of his resurrection, and may share his sufferings, becoming like him in his death,
¹¹ that by any means possible I may attain the resurrection from the dead."
Philippians 3 v 7-11 (ESV)

AMEN

Amen, amen ~
So it is that now these words,
Written down as testimony,
To all that is the wonder ~
Of the living Holy presence of our God.
They are also released into the great void.

Time and time and time again.
Eternity has its own momentum.
Bringing all the fullness of the will of God.

The journey continues,
And so it will be ~
The wilderness experience,
Yet holds more in its sway.
Wind and sand ~
Desolation to test the weary heart.

He will not ever leave us,
Neither does time allow our hasty exit.

His purposes will be fulfilled.
The Church of Jesus Christ enriched.
And glory, glory glory ~
Will be ~
Released once more.

When the windows of heaven are opened,
Then we will know,
Oh, how we will see ~

This precious life of the Holy Spirit,
Poured out,
As a rushing mighty stream.

It is a heavenly wonder,
Do you yearn for it so to be?
Are you groaning in your deepest heart experience?
Knocking on the doors of heaven.

Be still and know that He is God.
Be still and let your heart go free.

Be still ~
Oh, be still ~
Wait upon HIM.

Allowing His glorious freshness,
To saturate your life, your soul.
Until you are soaked ~
Immersed into HIM!

I am,
A voice in the wilderness,
My voice ~
Carried upon heavenly winds ~
Speaking to you of the wonders of heaven.
Hold out your hands,
Open your heart ~

He is the Lord of Glory,
Beautiful He is!
Wait upon His wonderful presence,
Be still ~
Be still.

All the ways of men,
The hardness of the road.
Do not stop here,
Forever it will continue so to be.

Only the opening of His will and His purpose,
These are the focus now

It is all of His will,
All of the purposes of heaven,
For His church and His people ~
To know,
To walk ~
In this golden pathway of blessing.

"In the six hundredth year of Noah's life, in the second month, on the seventeenth day of the month, on that day all the fountains of the great deep burst forth, and the windows of the heavens were opened."
Genesis 7 v 11 (ESV)

A time has been eternally set,
The hour, the day ~
It is held and waiting.

Will we and can we fulfil,
Those heavenly requirements?
To open a door ~
That has long been closed.

Opening the portals of heaven,
Bringing forth,
The River of God,
Upon our waiting hearts.

Reviving the church,
Bringing in the lost,
Sending forth ~
Labourers to sow good seed.

Then our nets will be filled,
Full and bursting.
A golden catch.

"Depart from me!"
Sinners will cry
"What is this?"
Troubled hearts will declare.

And now the church will arise,
Strong in the fullness of God.
Filled with the Holy Spirit.

Declaring the word of God,
Speaking truth,
As no man can stand to hear.

Condemning sin and unbelief.
This is a new way ~
A living way of power.

It is given,
To His church ~
His people.
For the bringing in of the lost,

Revival will come.
It is accomplished.
The Lord will opened heaven,
Pouring upon us
The wonders of grace.
Mercy flowing down like rivers.

Wonder of wonders,
Glory, Glory. Glory.

It is all of HIM.

AMEN.

THE WILDERNESS JOURNEY

The wilderness journey is set and there is no indication of where and when all will become fulfilled. Only this we can be certain to know, it is a way established by God and in God, where we are called to continue in obedience and trust.

Therefore it is, that now in the closing pages of this book, already He has established a further opening where the wilderness way opens up into new frontiers of understanding and the soul is illuminated by grace.

The barren and empty journey brings to the open heart new horizons and there is the imprinted hand of bright hope opening like a beautiful flower upon the dust and sand of emptiness. Journey with me into unknown revelations as grace is lavished upon what was thought to be a very empty way of desert.

To be continued...

- "THE SONG OF THE AGES:

  The song of the ages, is the song which the angels were heard to sing at the birth of Christ. This is the song that shepherds heard and were amazed, it is the very song of heaven. The Holy Spirit carries across eternity, the heavenly song, it is forever there to hear and even to join, as we open our hearts to God. These pages are written to reflect that heavenly touch upon a listening heart in a time of wilderness experience. When all else is removed, what do we have to sustain our way?

- THE GOSSAMER THREAD.

  As we listen to the heavenly voice, there is the finest thread moving across eternity, suddenly it is there and we hear and know that the Holy Spirit has touched once more our lives. Like a gossamer thread it passes across our way, are we listening and searching to know this touch of heaven? This is a book which takes the reader through a series of glimpses into the glorious potential of the life surrendered to the Lord Jesus Christ. We have found Him who is our Saviour, our Gracious Lord, but do not stop there, be ready and willing to arise and move on. It is His good pleasure to open up before us the wonders of heaven and to lead us along golden pathways upon which we have not yet tread, or even caught sight of.

www.ingramcontent.com/pod-product-compliance
Lightning Source LLC
Chambersburg PA
CBHW071629080526
44588CB00010B/1337